Saul
Anton

Saul Anton

Warhol's Dream

Edited by Xavier Douroux

Contents

Here's one for the Dream Syndicate: Picture Andy Warhol—silver wig, black turtleneck, the works—waiting a small eternity for Robert Smithson to cross the threshold of an elevator to the Empire State Building. The two have spent the morning trawling a deserted stretch of midtown Manhattan; and, naturally, their conversation has turned to that most sublime icon of New York architecture. A trip to the building's observation deck is in order.

Along the way—and to his surprise—Warhol learns that Smithson is more than a little phobic about elevators, which variously rouse feelings of claustrophobia and dread for the younger artist. The back-and-forth that anticipates this moment—a conversation that ranges from Warhol's virtually motionless, eight hour film of that very building, *Empire*; to Smithson's increasingly vertiginous theories of Ultramoderne architecture; to the land artist's proposition that Warhol start a rug factory—seems no less absurd than the circumstances that prompted the dialogue: a chance encounter at Warhol's favorite diner, the Star Palace, completely void of human presence save for the man Warhol calls "the best nowhere artist" he knows.

This is but one of the bizarre scenarios Saul Anton has conjured in *Warhol's Dream*, a fictional dialogue staged between Smithson and his at once perplexed and bemused interlocutor. And it is, of course, a dream—both a discursive and aerobic ramble that sees the two through New York city, culminating with a strange tête-à-tête in Central Park. In calling this conversation a dream, Anton wreaks havoc with a narrative device popular to sit-coms and made-for-TV movies: the moment when the hero awakens to discover that the remarkable turn of events just transpired is *only a dream*. "The strangest thing about this dream—what else could it have been?—Warhol himself suggests, is its clarity of detail: the fact that every last word of this Smithsonian conversation is recalled with the fidelity of his trusty SONY tape recorder. And so it goes for this book, which borrows liberally from the archives of Smithson and Warhol as much as it spins their peculiar syntax in its own phantasmatic direction.

At first blush, an imagined meeting between arguably the most influential artists of the 1960s reads as inspired parody, as if the darkly brooding Smithson—best known for producing work in the most remote of sites—played the titular straight man (or intellectual foil) to Warhol, always dispatching his witticisms with bland indifference; and always at the eye of the social hurricane. And you would not be wrong to call *Warhol's Dream* a deftly fashioned and very funny parody, dazzling in Anton's capacity to mime the rhetorical habits of both artists. No doubt, Anton has read closely—even internalized—the writings of Warhol and Smithson. His feel for their patterns of speech, their solecisms and cadences, is uncanny. The art historian of the period, however, understands that a dialogue between the two is to the point, and not only because Smithson paid homage to Warhol on more than one textual and artistic occasion; and not only because they rubbed elbows with some frequency down at Max's Kansas City. Their various writings, to say little of their sculptures, photographs, silkscreens, and films, have played no small role in the language of contemporary theories of art and art writing. We are in absolute thrall to their critical legacy.

Yet one need only scratch the surface of *Warhol's Dream* to see that Anton's project goes well beyond showcasing an enviable gift for ventriloquism as well as the concerns of Art History proper. In fact I want to call it a demonstration piece of the "Metalogic Imagination," suggesting the impossible (because imaginary and dreamlike) dimensions of the conversation itself. Readers with a taste for literary theory might hear in this phrase the ring of the Russian formalist Mikhail Bakhtin, whose notion of the "dialogic imagination" or novelistic discourse, broadly understood language to be a dialogic operation, ever open to the conditions of heteroglossia in contrast to the straitjacket functionalism of grammar. The "metalogic imagination" stands to trump Bakhtin's dialogism in turn: it troubles further the presumptions we make about dialogues in the first place. Indeed, in everyday speech, we place faith in the structure of the dialogue for its putative revelation of information; the generation of discourse; the achievement of consensus through the reasoned communication of its participants. A dialogue, we imagine, performs the concrete work of the dialectic. Through the engagement of two speakers, critical theses are hypothesized, contradicted, debated, and resolved.

But there is no such resolution between Warhol and Smithson, only a conversational volley that goes on from the subject of death to the movies to the fear of time to Richard Nixon. In calling this endless reflection "metalogic" I borrow from the influential anthropologist and cybernetician Gregory Bateson, who knew a thing or two about that acutely contemporary notion of the dialogue, feedback. Bateson defined the metalogue in the following terms:

> A metalogue is a conversation about some problematic subject. This conversation should be such that not only do the participants discuss the problem but the structure of the conversation as a whole is also relevant to the same subject.[1]

A metalogue, in other words, reproduces the subject of a dialogue at the level of its form. The structure becomes a mirror to the topic introduced. And what gets reproduced in this exchange—what may or may not be adequately communicated or translated between "form" and "content"—goes to the ambitions of criticism itself, its viability and continued relevance. (Here, as Reinhold Koselleck reminds us, we need recall that modern criticism finds its genealogy in the rhetoric of the emergency room, as if criticism—linked to the sense of a medical crisis—functioned as a strategic intervention, a type of "life-or-death" decision). The form of the metalogue, however, complicates this idea through the logic of its internal reproduction. It stages the crisis of critical discourse, though it may not be clear whether with the intent to resuscitate or to kill criticism. Or, to put this in a less dramatic way: Is the critical form of a metalogue a transparent medium of communication—transparent in making the goals of the dialogue plain? Or rather, is it a communicative *mise en abyme*—a recursive hall of mirrors given over to endless echoes and ever multiplying reflections, a dialogue never to resolve itself?

This is not the usual stuff of art history, to be sure. When we think of these questions—if we think of them at all—we tend to consult a Derrida or a Jean-Luc Nancy whether on the buried metaphysics of the speech act or on a theory of community founded on infinite (and necessarily failed) conversation. Yet with an academic training in modern critical theory and aesthetics, Anton knows the lay of this land very well. In Warhol and Smithson, he has recognized fellow travelers in their respective attitudes to criticism. One of the merits of *Warhol's Dream* is that it reveals the artists to be doppelgangers of a type, whatever their ostensible differences in style and approach. More often than not, the convergence between the two rests with the problematic of criticality and communicative mediation. Take, for instance, the "Death and Disaster" series by Warhol, which reflect on the limits of representation in their blank-faced depictions of trauma. Or consider the theory of entropy elaborated by Smithson, which articulates the disintegration of a message ("energy drain") as it is subjected to the vagaries of communication. It is in this sense that the form of a dream-like dialogue between the two is a mirror to their own theoretical pursuits: the dream of criticality in general. That the trope of the mirror and endless reflection is so vital to both artists is itself in keeping with the structural bases of the metalogue —a mirror to the topic under discussion.

To push this conceit even further, *Warhol's Dream* bears little pretension to reinvent the wheel for art criticism. Instead, it takes repetition and reproducibility as both the generative mechanism of criticism *and* its potential aporia. The Warhol acolyte immediately recognizes Anton's book to be both homage and mirror of another sort: a mirror to Warhol's own *The Philosophy of Andy Warhol: From A to B and Back again* (1975). This summa of Warholian banality was loosely based on "transcripts" of taped phone conversations between Warhol and the redoubtable Brigid Polk. (Anton, for his part, swaps the "B" of Brigid Polk with the "B" of Bob Smithson.) And the dialogical structure of *The Philosophy of Andy Warhol*, which unfolds with the narrative tension of the Pittsburgh Yellow Pages, is a mirror—or rather, a faintly heard echo— in another sense. For the book reads like an echo of the 1960s, a time in which, as Warhol puts it "everybody got interested in everybody." This he opposed to the time in which he "wrote" *The Philosophy*—the 1970s—the moment when "*everybody started dropping everybody.*"

You could read this as an allegory of criticism, the historical point at which an interest in "everybody" (a public, so to speak) gave way to the evacuation of all social discourse, a veritable "dropping" of the world. Not that this was a new topic for Warhol by any means. As one of the canniest observers of the burgeoning information society—the endless horizon of television, film, print journalism, computers—Warhol's work was always enmeshed in, and always questioning of, the relative powers of communications media and the utopian dream of its pure and utter transparency. At roughly the same moment that Jürgen Habermas was advancing his theories of the public sphere in Germany, Warhol, in his own fashion, was challenging the viability of that sphere at the Factory, the Dom, and the Filmmakers Cinematheque. Typically, though, Warhol made ample use of the media alleged to debase that very communicative sensibility. Smithson was no slouch in this department either. To flip through the pages of his collected writings is to confront, over and over again, what he saw as the recursive logic of art and media in general, what he deemed "reproduced reproductions" in his important essay "Quasi-Infinities and the Waning of Space." Like Warhol, Smithson understood it as axiomatic that the fullness of any type of "message," be it a piece of art criticism or a work of art, was contingent upon the peculiar form of reproduction it took; and where, in turn, that reproduction was sited in space and time.

Anton will mine this tradition even further back in history. Apart from the model of "criticism" proposed by Warhol, the structure of his dialogue finds its touchstone in much older prototypes: think, for instance, of Mondrian's trialogues on abstraction or Paul Valery' Socratic exchanges set in the Elysian fields. Above all, Anton harkens back to the example set by Enlightenment aesthetics in the form of Denis Diderot's Salon dialogues. Diderot, who might well be called the father of modern art criticism, probed the limits of a criticism he was himself inventing, dramatizing what is necessarily partial in all matters of aesthetic judgment.

And far in advance of so many bad television shows, Diderot deployed the form of the "dream" narrative to make his points about criticism, too. Listen to this imaginary exchange between a connoisseur and an ordinary woman, untutored in the business of what counts as good art:

"Do you like this painting?"

"No, not at all."

"But, why not? It's a Raphael?"

"Well, that may be, but I think your Raphael is an idiot."

"Whatever makes you say that?"

"Isn't that supposed to be the Holy Virgin?"

"That's right, and that's the Christ Child with her,"

"Well, of course. But who's the other baby there?"

"That's Saint John."

"So it is. Now how old would you say Jesus is?"

"Fifteen, eighteen months?"

"And Saint John?"

"Four or five years old?"

"Oh, I see … Then why does the Bible say that both mothers were pregnant at the same time?" [2]

The punch line, of course, is that no matter how reasoned and logical the position of the "average" woman, it does nothing to sway the opinion of the art expert, who takes sides with Raphael regardless of the Renaissance master's demands on our credulity.

Anton is at once faithful to the spirit of this tradition as well as rightfully skeptical of its imperatives. He is not the slavish heir apparent to this genre of writing. Some two hundred years plus separate the moment of Diderot's *Salons* from ours, after all; and while it's self-flattering to imagine that contemporary writing on art carries a polemical charge equal to the founding moment of art criticism, the more recent fate of public discourse suggests otherwise. The reasons why this is so are far too complicated to do justice to in this context, but no matter how you parse the phenomenon, one thing is clear: there are very few "standout" internecine battles being waged in the trenches of art criticism today, no modern day Goethes, Diderots, or Lessings to take up the cause.

Given this seemingly sad state of affairs, one might ask to what end is Anton recasting this venerable critical tradition? In the case of Warhol and Smithson, a dialogue of this order is only doomed to fail; it can only take place in a dream as such. Here, then, two moments in Anton's dialogue grant special insight into the metalogic imagination. The first, occasioned by a glimpse at the Empire State Building, is an oblique commentary on criticism's modeling of, or intervention into, history:

> B   A famous critic once wrote that it was a matter of "brushing history against the grain." He meant that we need to understand it in ways that it never understood itself …

> A   … I've always thought it's not worth it to brush things against the grain, because the problem is how everyone else takes what you do once you've done it. The minute someone starts to get it, they start to copy it. Then, all of the sudden, instead of brushing against the grain, you're going with the flow.

Thus Warhol suggests (if in his own way) that the dialectical gesture of "brushing history against the grain"—one of the methodological hallmarks of modern criticism—is little more than a Benjaminian flip-flop: always in danger of being copied, reproduced, and assimilated into the "flow."

Another passage—both hilarious and serious—brings us even more abruptly to the heart of the matter for criticism. In an exchange about the movement between uptown socialites and downtown habitués—the rarefied climes of Madison Avenue and the demi-monde of the Factory—Smithson trots out one of his favorite turns-of-phrase. "It's dialectical," he opines, to which Warhol responds with strange vehemence: "Will you please stop using that word."

Warhol would put an end to Smithson's use of the word "dialectical." He would stop the dialectic (and all it implies for criticism, for history, and for the historicity of criticism, dead in its tracks. And that desire to "end" the dialectic—a certain refusal to move toward critical resolution—is its own kind of non-eventfulness or death, which sheds light on the continued project of art criticism and the recognition of its failures (and failure as one of its necessary conditions). It's in keeping with one of the key topics of the dialogue itself. Metalogically speaking, the subject of death haunts the discussion between Warhol and Smithson. Warhol, in fact, is convinced that both are actually dead, a realization that doesn't really seem to trouble either artist too much in the strange and timeless place in which they find themselves.

It is precisely this "Non-Site" of the critical wilderness that Anton maps so skillfully in *Warhol's Dream*. As an art critic, he knows too well the stakes, foibles, and dreams of the very enterprise to which he repeatedly returns. You have to wonder: who is dreaming whom? Anton on Warhol? Warhol on Smithson? Smithson on all of us? Perhaps it is only fair that Warhol have the last word on the topic. Until, of course, there is another last word:

> The annoying thing is that whenever people hear the word "art," they start acting like lawyers. Whenever you mention that word, they start getting very stiff and nervous, and begin asking what you mean, as if you were signing a contract and they wanted to know what you mean when you say you're going to "pay" them a thousand dollars. Critics are the worst. I guess it's their job, but you say one word and they start asking what you mean, but if you ask them the same thing, they behave as if they've said the most obvious thing in the world. If I were a critic, I would worry about my words rather than what artists mean when they talk.

Pamela M. Lee

Notes

[1]
Gregory Bateson, *Steps to an Ecology of Mind*
(Chandler Publishing for Health Sciences,
San Fransisco, 1972), p .2.

[2]
Cited in Udo Kultermann, *The History of Art
History*, (Abaris Books, New York, 1993), p. 31.
For the original French version, see Denis
Diderot, *Pensées détachées sur la peinture, la
sculpture, l'architecture et la poésie, pour servir de
suite aux* Salons, in *Héros et Martyrs*, (Hermann,
Paris, 1995), p. 398.

Let attention be paid not to the matter but to the shape I give it.
—Michel de Montaigne

Empire

It was a terrible night. The phone started ringing at 4 am, and everytime I picked it up, no one was there. It took me an hour and a Seconal to fall asleep, but at 6 am. the same thing happened all over again. This time, I couldn't fall asleep, so after tossing and turning for an hour, I called Brigid and asked her if she'd called me and hung up. She said she'd been out until four and that she'd been thinking about me all night, but that she'd never do a thing like that. She said she thought I'd been in a strange mood when I went home after the party for Liz Taylor's new movie, and she wondered if her thoughts about me had made my phone ring. I said I didn't think so and told her she better not lie because I knew it was her. Her answer was that she wouldn't be in until the afternoon, so I told her to just take the whole day off.

Getting a phone call and finding no one on the line is one of the most disappointing things that can happen in life. If you ever bother to call someone, you should be obligated to talk to them. If you've got nothing to say, you should find something—even if it's just that you liked what they were wearing the last time you saw them. Otherwise, you're not only wasting their time, you're also letting them know that you don't have anything to say to them.

I decided to get some breakfast, so I got myself together and went out. What was strange was that there was no one on the street. It was totally deserted. Wow, I thought, this is exactly what it's like early on Sunday mornings when the weather's bad and when no one wants to get up. You can walk all over town and have the streets to yourself. But on this day, the weather was beautiful. First I get a prank call; now I went over to Madison, and it was something to see all those stores closed. Imagine strolling down the Avenue without having to stop for people, get out of their way, or squeeze in behind them to look in the windows. For a moment, I didn't know what to do with myself. Where was everyone? I headed up to the Star Palace, my favorite diner, on the corner of 37th Street, and I was very happy when I saw that it was open. After breakfast, I thought, I'd just show up at the Factory and surprise everyone, since I haven't been getting there as early as I used to.

But when I went into the diner, who did I see sitting in the back booth, but Robert Smithson. The day really was getting stranger because I hadn't even seen the corner hot dog man at his usual spot. Bob's not someone you see around a lot. These days, he doesn't come by the Factory as much as he used to. He's always out West doing whatever he does, or wandering around New Jersey or Mexico looking for places that no one can find. The last time I saw him, he told me he was trying to buy an island somewhere. I said, "You're already on an island."

Bob did that piece out West on the Salt Lake. Ever since Brigid saw the pictures they published in that little art magazine—I always forget the name—she calls him the "nowhere" man. She thinks that the whole point of art is for it to be somewhere so people could come and see it, but that Smithson was trying to force us to have to leave New York and go out to the middle of nowhere. I could see her point, so I told her I thought he was the best nowhere artist I knew, and that, after all, even nowhere needed art. After that, she warmed up to him, and I even saw them talking and smoking cigarettes at our parties. Both of them like to smoke a lot and like to talk about smoking I've always thought people smoked so they didn't have to talk.

Anyway, there he was sitting in the corner booth by the window, looking like he'd been waiting for me all along. I've always thought he was very polite. He would always come over to say hello when he came by. A lot of people don't bother. I guess if he comes by at all, that means he's not that shy. He was always telling me that he really liked my movies and that I was "really onto something," but that I had to stop listening to all the people around me who were trying to make me into an "art film" director. I remember how he said "onto something," and how he said "art film" like it was the worst thing in the world. I even asked him once what he had against "art film." He answered: "nothing, only so long as they don't try to make the actors act." I agree. Acting is really boring to watch. It's much better when the actor doesn't do anything. Bob also liked to tell me that he'd made a couple of films himself and that he thought it would be great if I could be in one of his movies someday. "Don't worry, you don't have to say anything unless you want to," he said. I remember that very clearly, even though I never figured out why he'd asked since the films of his that I had seen hardly had people in them.

I can't remember how I answered him. I probably just said "sure." That's what I say to almost everything. "Sure" is the surest word you can use because it doesn't mean *yes* and it doesn't mean *no*. People are always disappointed if you tell them no, so I try not to; on the other hand, you can't say yes, either, because they usually take it to mean something other than what you mean. "Sure" doesn't really mean "maybe," either. It just means "sure," which is anything they want it to mean, but a meaning that they can't hold you to. "Sure" is the most artistic word I know. It's probably even more artistic than the word "art." That's how people should deal with each other. You can take whatever meaning you want from it, but that doesn't mean you can hold me to it.

The annoying thing is that whenever people hear the word "art," they start acting like lawyers. Whenever you mention that word, they start getting very stiff and nervous, and begin asking you what you mean, as if you were signing a contract and they wanted to know what you mean when you say you're going to "pay" them a thousand dollars. Critics are the worst. I guess it's their job, but you say one word and they start asking you what you mean, but if you ask them the same thing, they behave as if they've said the most obvious thing in the world. If I were a critic, I would worry about my words rather than the artist's words. Everyone knows they'll say just about anything, anyway.

Bob writes a lot, but he's never stiff and he always knows what he means, even if you don't. In fact, a lot of the time, he stands around using words you've never heard of, trying to tell you what they mean. That's really why I like him, I guess, even though that's exactly why a lot of people don't like him. They think he's an "intellectual." And if they do like him, it's only because they think he's a great artist. Everyone says he's a great artist. Either way, it's always fun to invite him over, because he's always making fun of people who don't realize that's what he's doing. I like to see him do that because it's not like how anyone else I know does it.

But it's a shame he only gets into the art magazines. I think they should put him on the cover of *Time* or another big magazine like that. His work is big and it's made not only for New York people but for everyone, like roller coasters or something like that. Of course, I know they won't because he's probably too weird. You can't be too weird if you want to be on the cover of *Time*, or if you are, you have to be weird in the way they want you to be weird, like a murderer, a cult leader, a communist rebel, or someone like that, which isn't really weird because anyone can see any of those characters on TV any night of the week. No one notices people who are really weird. They only notice people who are weird in a way they can understand, which also means that the weirdos they do notice are just acting. Maybe that's the weirdest thing of all, people who aren't weird acting weird. Really weird people never think they're weird. I guess that's why Bob is really weird: no one thinks he is. They all think he's a genius, even though they've seen his work mostly in magazines. (I've been trying to do that for years now, but can't seem to get the hang of it. Clients always want to come over for lunch. Who ever said that when you commission a portrait, you get lunch with it?)

Brigid and Gregory Battcock like to sit around and read his articles aloud for anyone who's around and when they're finished I flip through the pictures. No one really understands what he is getting at, but everyone really likes hearing his articles read aloud. They all say Bob has a way with words. Brigid said that one day, and then everyone started to repeat it. I wouldn't know really. I guess I don't know much about words. All I can say is Bob really likes to get his hands dirty. He's always talking about crystals, stars, galaxies, dinosaurs, rockets, philosophy, and who knows what else. I stand there and listen for a while, until Fred or Pat or someone else comes to tell me I have a phone call.

And there he was now, sitting there, the only person in the whole place, with a cup of tea in front of him, looking like he'd been expecting me. I was all alone, too, without even my Sony. I started getting paranoid that maybe I had made an appointment with Bob and had forgotten about it, so I was thinking of all the things I would say to Brigid for not reminding me, but then I remembered it was barely eight in the morning. No matter how hard I try, I just have no mind for time. So there we were, just the two of us, with no one else in the place.

I walked up and sat down across from him like John Wayne and said, "Hello Bob." He just laughed, and said, "Don't be such a formalist." I knew he was joking, because I'd heard him say that to other people before. He could be pretty funny when he wanted to, even though that was a pretty bad joke, the kind abstract painters tease each other with. So I said I didn't know what he meant, and he kept smiling, like he'd known all along what I would say. I started to think of something else to say, but then, out of the blue, he asked if I wanted to go with him to the planetarium.

Everything was already pretty strange, but I was trying to act like everything was normal. What else could I do? We hadn't even said hello and we were acting like we had seen each other an hour ago and were picking up the conversation again in the middle—which is usually where my B decides to say something and saves me the trouble. But here there was no B.

"What's there to see there?" I asked.

"A lot. Rocks and dioramas of rocks, and dinosaurs, of course. Entire strata spanning millions of years of life on Earth."

"That's not much fun to look at," I said.

He laughed again:

"Okay. Then how about going up to the observation deck of the Empire State Building? It's a clear blue sky today, so we'll be able to see very far."

I hadn't been expecting the question, or him, and I really didn't know what to say. I couldn't remember the last time I'd been there (it must have been in the 50s). So I just said, "Sure."

"Great. We can go right now if you're ready."

"Usually, when I want to see something far away, I see it on television."

"Television?"

"Sure. Don't you think the observation deck is obsolete now? TV lets you see more things farther away, especially if it's cloudy."

"Probably, but it's not the same."

The strangest thing about this dream—what else could it have been?— is that I remember the entire afternoon in perfect detail. I even knew at that very moment that somehow I didn't need my Sony to record it. I would remember all of it word for word and second by second. It was as if we were in a movie—which was fine by me.

Bob So, you really want to go?

Andy I just said so, didn't I? Fifth Avenue is my second-favorite avenue.

Bob Which one's your favorite?

Andy Madison.

Bob Why is that?

Andy All of the fashion boutiques. I couldn't buy most of that stuff, but I always love a good shop window. Lower Fifth is nice too. On weekends, it's deserted. Everyone's uptown at Bergdorf's and Bloomingdale's, and only a few are down here looking for rugs.

Bob It doesn't seem like we have to worry about any crowds today.

Andy Well, it's still pretty early. Are you sure they'll let us go up at this hour?

Bob I don't see why not.

Andy Anyway, what I was going to say was that when you think about it, the rug stores are just like art galleries, aren't they? They have those giant silk carpets in the windows wall-to-wall, the way I did my cows, and in the big stores, you almost feel like you're in a museum. You don't even have to pay for admission.

Bob I see what you mean. Are you ready?

We got up and left without even paying the bill. But there was no one there, so it didn't seem like it mattered. Outside we headed over to Fifth, and on the way over, we passed one of those large imported rug emporiums I had just been talking about.

Andy Aren't they fantastic?

Bob Some of the rugs are the result of hundreds of years of work, so we really have no idea what we're looking at or who the artist was.

Andy I didn't know that.

Bob It's like looking at a Gothic cathedral. You're not seeing the execution of a blue-print; rather, you're seeing a series of evolutions that don't necessarily make sense together. We think we're seeing just a pattern or a picture, but we're really looking at cross-sections of time, cathedrals in wool and silk, a weave of conflicting ideas and priorities.

Andy Not to mention jealousies, illnesses, and that sort of thing. That's how things work when you run a large studio. B becomes jealous of C, so they start doing everything totally differently, then they get sick, and C has to figure out what's going on. People always try so hard to control everything that happens in their work.

Bob It's part of the process.

Andy I say the less control the better. In the very beginning, I tried really hard to control what was happening, and I kept catching a cold. So I had to stop trying so hard, and I realized that's what I ought to do. Everyone's happy to do the work and more work gets done, which is really the most important thing. Except I once told Lou Reed when he showed up and announced he'd written ten songs that week that he ought to have written 15.

Bob What happened?

Andy He didn't like that.

Bob You know Andy, I can easily imagine you doing a rug series—large silkscreens of designs from all over the world—Mexico, Morocco, Egypt, Turkey, Iran. Aren't you tired of Americana? Why not explore other countries? One day you could have factories in Marrakesh, Istanbul, Mexico City, Kabul, Teheran—wherever they make rugs.

Andy That's an interesting idea, but I've always thought of myself as an American artist.

Bob Instead of one Factory, you'd have many factories. Instead of one artist, you would be many, many artists.

Andy If I ever go international, I'd like to do it in the American way, like McDonald's.

Bob You'd transform your business art into an international brand.

Andy I don't think we could sell too many rugs. They look great in windows, but if I started hanging them on the wall, I think I'd stop liking them. Maybe it needs to be something other than rugs.

Bob Like what?

Andy Like maybe those camouflage uniforms soldiers wear. They're more modern.

Bob Is that how you chose your other icons, like the soup cans and the dollar bills? You started with one thing and then you found something like it that you liked better?

Andy Not really. You can't live without soup or money or movie stars, not in this country. But a rug? Well, you can take it or leave it. Carpets are more practical. Rugs I like when they're just hanging in shop windows. What would I look at when I'm coming down Fifth Avenue?

Bob You could make them really big, even fill the entire gallery wall, like your cow patterns.

Andy It sounds like an idea you'd like to do.

All of a sudden, the Empire State loomed over us.

Bob I thought you said you don't like to control things too much. If I worked for you, you wouldn't let me make rug paintings?

Andy Just imagine how much carpeting the Empire State Building needs. A hundred floors times who knows how many square feet. Maybe ten thousand per floor. That's a million square feet of floor space that needs carpeting.

Bob The Empire State building is one of the few structures in this city that challenges the idea that man is the measure of all things. It transcends the anthropomorphism that forms the foundation for modern art even at its most abstract.

Andy It's very impressive.

Bob To bring it somehow into the gallery would be to make the non-site of non-sites, one hundred unimaginable floors that one would have to wander through.

Andy That's a great idea. You could use one of those new video cameras.

Bob That's not what I mean.

Andy It's a lot of space. Imagine the party you could throw if you could get them to give you the whole building.

Bob The Empire State is not merely a work of architecture. It's a great space-time machine. It recalls the prehistoric and allows us to imagine a different future.

Andy We're almost there. I always forget how close by it is. Probably because most of the time I forget to look up. I don't think I've been there since the 1950s.

Bob You didn't go up before you made *Empire?*

Andy No. Do you think we should have?

Bob It might have given you a different perspective.

Andy But we didn't want perspective.

Bob Well, look up today, because it looks like the sky is so clear that we'll have the full effect, especially with the sun rising higher now.

Andy What kind of perspective do you think we'll get?

Bob If we walked around the building once before we went up, we could see it from every direction.

Andy Sure.

At that moment, Bob put on these sunglasses, the ones he wore in his spiral movie. All the kids at the Factory think they're awful, but not me. I thought he looked pretty good in them. We turned on 34th Street and started walking towards Macy's, and Bob started to look up. I did, too, but then I strained my neck. I didn't think it's a building meant to be seen from up close, so I started to just look at Macy's, which was a lot easier to look at. As we came nearer, I realized that it was closed, even though it was after eight. Maybe they had changed their hours, I thought.

Bob Unlike the Pyramids of Egypt, the ziggurats, or even the tiered buildings from the 1920s and 30s, the Empire State Building doesn't recede from you, nor does it allow your eye to approach it.

Andy But what about the antenna? It's hard to see if you're standing right under it.

Bob Exactly. It forces you to stand a certain distance away. It doesn't mimic perspective, as if it wished it could disappear into a hole in the sky, the way the Pyramids do.

I looked up again and couldn't see the point at the top. Whew, I thought. I'd only been guessing. But when he mentioned ziggurats, my heart almost stopped.

Andy We went to Mexico a few years ago and visited one of those. Bob Colacello and Fred wanted me to climb it, but I decided to stay in the car while they went up. A few minutes later, I was surrounded by hundreds of people, all of whom were staring at me. The driver turned off the air-conditioning so the car wouldn't overheat, so I started to sweat into my suit. By the time they got back, I was a little upset. They'd brought me a souvenir, but I said it was just a pile of rocks. I would never say that about the Empire State. Still, the word "ziggurat" gets to me. I don't think my glands will ever forget that day and when I hear that word I just start to sweat.

Bob Instead of remembering, you should forget, because it's not very hot today.

Andy True.

Bob Can you see the antenna needle on top?

Andy Not from here.

Bob It's as if the building has taken over the entire sky, as if it were saying that no matter how far up you go, you're still in the anthroposphere.

Andy What sphere?

Bob In the same way New York keeps going far beyond Manhattan, the Empire State extends the borders of the human sphere upward and claims the sky as part of the human realm. That's why New York is really the only truly international city. Being international is not just about moving across the globe. Expansion presumes that one has already conquered the sky. The Empire State is a universal artwork. It claims the heavens in the name of mankind.

I looked up again and could see exactly what Bob was talking about. The Empire State stood over you, and looked like it was floating in the sky, not like it was standing on the ground. It was like the face of a movie star on a billboard, only bigger than any billboard could ever be. When we arrived at the corner of 6th Avenue, we could see its entire Western face all the way up to the needle.

Andy That's true, except on rainy days, when the needle disappears into the clouds.

Bob Its design is exactly contrary to that of the Pyramids, which clearly marked the limit of the human sphere by offering a perspective point that disappears into the sky. Standing at the bottom, you're never denied a line of sight. The Pyramids suggest that even the pharaohs, who towered above mortals as the representatives of the gods, were still only emanations of the divine, and still subject to the infinite, into which they returned once their earthly reign came to an end.

Andy What I really like about the Pyramids is that they're all the same. The only thing that ever changed was their size. You can't say that about cathedrals. They couldn't even finish one of those without changing the style halfway though.

Bob Like making a rug but changing the design as you go.

Andy Exactly.

Bob But there's really no way to avoid that if it takes a hundred and fifty years to build something. You can't cancel time.

Andy What about the Pyramids? I think they figured if they were going to build monuments to the dead, they should probably come up with a good design and stick with it. That's how I would do it. Otherwise, people never know what death looks like, and that's very important. That's what we have the news for.

Bob had this far-away look, the kind that Billy Name would get sometimes before he disappeared into the darkroom. We came around on 33rd Street and started walking back toward Fifth Avenue. The sun was rising in front of us, and I realized that's why Bob had put on his sunglasses. Of course, I'd left mine at home, which is what I always do because I never think that it will be sunny out. It was then that I noticed how silent the city was, like someone had turned off all the sound. There weren't any cars or buses or shoppers. Not even any Chinese food delivery men.

Bob A funerary structure is by default about transcendence, yet neither the Egyptians nor the pre-Colombians believed in artistic expression. It was just where the God lived. The West, on the other hand, has always been insecure about its relation to the Godhead and how best to express it. Our symbolic systems are merely strata of failed attempts to nail down transcendence. Modern communications media are just the latest form of it.

Andy Symbols are too complicated for me, but then I guess people are symbolizing all the time, especially on television.

Bob Even the Empire State is a part of that history, though it might actually mark its end. It's an intriguing idea to toy with.

Andy You think the Empire State is a failure?

Bob As an icon, it's on a par with anything, but as a structure, it deviates significantly from its ideal. Mostly, because its sheer material enormity transcends its architectural ideals and begins to impinge on its surroundings.

Andy I thought they meant to build it that big. You mean they didn't?

Bob Let me give you an example. The sun is still far off from its zenith, so at the moment the Fifth Avenue side gets most of the light while the Sixth Avenue side is in the shade. In a few hours, the reverse will occur. These kinds of extreme contrasts create imbalances, hollows, and whirlpools in the normal warp and woof of natural conditions that cause displacement and rapid transformation. The long-term effect of extended shadows, more the product of memory and habit than perception, has been the grand collapse of the American ideal of the picturesque. New York as an entity has by now completely submitted itself to this condition.

Andy I don't have a very good memory, so I try avoid using a lot of shadows and try to draw things as directly as I can. I even draw shadows that way.

Bob The sun rises at a different angle every single day, and forces us to adjust ourselves ever so slightly. So there's no such thing as direct perception.

Andy True, but summer or winter, the sun is the sun.

Bob The sun, Andy, is really a composite fiction of a trillion smaller explosions—a trillion suns we will never know.

Andy I remember that line from *Spiral Jetty*.

Bob We live and move in a heliocentric metaphor.

Andy I've never been much for the sun. Being indoors is easier. Lou once called me a vampire, thinking it would bother me. I like to watch television at night, but I'm definitely not a television vampire.

Bob Didn't you once say you only watch television in the daytime?

Andy Possibly. Sometimes I think that if I watch enough TV, I'll see all the images I'll ever need, and then I'll be done. In those moments, I want to watch more TV. Other times, I worry what I'd do if I did finish. What would replace television?

Bob You could never exhaust the world's images. The more images we see, the more we need.

Andy Why is that?

Bob People think a picture is a thousand words, but it's more like ten thousand images. In fact, you're the one who first demonstrated this proliferation *ad infinitum*.

Andy That's true, but I once I see an image of something, I become fixated and have a hard time liking any other picture of that thing. That's why I have to make each one a little different. I always do more pictures than I need, that way I can let others choose the one they prefer.

Bob The infinite is both more and less than just "more." Every variation suggests infinite possibilities. Architecture registers the actuality of this entropic imbalance, the infinity of every picture, by producing no pictures at all. In science fiction, they call it "energy drain."

Andy No pictures at all? What about gargoyles and stained glass and things like that?

Bob You have to remember that cathedrals were designed to be like books for the unlettered. That is no longer true. A basic structure produces no single image.

Andy Except maybe for the Empire State, don't you think?

Bob It's no accident that the Renaissance emerged after the collapse of the Gothic cathedral as the European artistic paradigm. Every innovation in art since then has been an attempt to rebuild what was destroyed, but plasticity alone can't knit the humpty dumpty medieval world back together again. Neither can what smarmy magazines peddle as "culture."

Andy If you ask me, even if it's off-balance, the Empire State is one of the great images of all time, one that's not going to run out of energy anytime soon. If I were its owner, I'd copyright it.

Bob Too much painting and sculpture today pretends that energy is evenly distributed across space and the world is composed of smooth surfaces and discrete substances. But the vortexes of light and shadow, the collapse of one plane of existence into another, have to be taken into account. Science fiction is aware of this, but neither architecture nor art take much notice.

Andy Why should they?

Bob For the simple reason that art "is" energy drain.

Andy I've never noticed that.

Bob Energy drain can be perceived only indirectly, in the infinitely small or what tries to be larger than the largest. It can also be perceived in the dust-filled volumes of the history of art.

We arrived at the southeast corner of the building, when, all of a sudden, a large cloud passed overhead and the sun disappeared for a moment.

Andy It's always much better to stand in the shade. Whenever I'm in the shade, I want to stay there. In the sun, everything gets so … um … clear. It's better when everything blends in more.

Bob I try not to see things in terms of those kinds of oppositions. Though you may think so, shade and sunlight are not opposites.

Andy No?

Bob We project symmetry onto a universe that's not symmetrical. Not even the Empire State can give the heavens symmetry, because the sky is not a place we can conquer with patterns and order.

Andy Rain or shine, it's the one thing that never stops working.

Bob Yes, but some day it might stop. It might even start running backward.

Andy I guess, but right now it's about to come out again, so are you ready to go up to the top?

Bob In a minute … Art does that all the time. It doesn't just move in one direction, and yet it has a kind of irreversibility.

Andy You mean it piles up.

Bob Literally. The Empire State is one place in New York where you're actually able to grasp this experientially.

Andy You mean it's a pile of rocks. Is it the only one?

Bob No, there are others. One place is the Museum of Natural History. There, history has literally become piles of rocks, which are then revived with "art." Another place is Central Park. But from the top of the

Empire State, the rivers must look like long sheets of glass, and New York harbor resembles a giant mirror in which the sky looks at itself. The rivers and the buildings know that this zone is generally forbidden to humans, but we still have to learn that. If it were up to me, I wouldn't let children up there, but I would make it mandatory for adults.

Andy Why?

Bob From up there, the smallest unit of cognition is probably the tree —or maybe the car. People fall below minimum levels of visibility. Even if you can see them, individuals become insignificant. History ossifies itself.

Andy I like to meet history before it becomes history.

Bob A famous critic once wrote that what was important was to "brush history against the grain."

Andy That's interesting.

Bob He meant we need to understand it in ways that it never understood itself—most of all, not just historically.

Andy Hmm …

Bob It's a matter of seeing rather than looking. When you're only looking, you're only looking at what you've been told to see out of habit. In that sense, it's better to remain here for a while and not rush to go up.

Andy I've always thought it's not worth brushing things against the grain. The real problem is how everyone else takes what you do once you've done it. The minute someone starts to get it, they copy you. Then, all of a sudden, instead of brushing against the grain, you're going with the flow.

Bob Just because someone has imitated you?

Andy Sure. It's better to just go with the flow, because it's harder for people to pick you out. That's what the Empire State building did, I think. It just went with the flow, like all the other skyscrapers. It might be taller and larger, but it's all about the look if you ask me.

Bob Andy, I've never known you to go with the flow.

Andy The truth is the art world is always trying to brush things against the grain, which is why it seems like I'm brushing against the grain. But I do just the opposite. I go with the flow, but everyone in the art world says I'm brushing against the grain.

Bob I get it.

Andy You know, you can now buy 3-D postcards of those new World Trade Centers in Gimbels. And last month, we went to a party at the top. The next day, I went and bought a whole set.

Bob What for?

Andy So that I could remember that I'd been there. Do you think they need to be brushed against the grain, too?

Bob Well, I'd start with the basic fact about the Twin Towers.

Andy What's that?

Bob The fact that there are two.

Andy If you ask me, I'd have built another Empire State instead of them. Then we could have had Twin Empire State Buildings. That way, it wouldn't go the way of the Woolworth building, which one day was the tallest building in the world, and the next day, it wasn't. *Poof!* Just like that. Who pays attention to the Woolworth building today? But if they had built another Woolworth building, that wouldn't have happened. It would be as famous as the Empire State building, and they wouldn't have even built the Twin Towers, since they would already have them.

Bob But even if they had, the Empire State would still have been taller. Even if that weren't true, two buildings still have the same problems as one—and twice over. A building still lives first in the mind, where one pictures being at the top a thousand times before one ever gets there. An yet, when one finally does get there, it's never what one imagined. It's not the triumph of man, but the evidence of his nullity. One stands there with a queasy feeling in one's stomach, thinking that it's just nerves responding to the great distances that seemed so serene and sublime on some postcard. In reality, it's the distance between the ideal and the reality that brings on the lightheadedness, not the actual height.

Andy I think that's true about movie stars, too. You dream about them for years—thinking about what you'll wear and what you'll say to them if you ever meet them. When you finally do, after five minutes of polite chitchat, they start complaining that they want to go to a different party.

Bob The Empire State is both stranger and more familiar than you ever can imagine. From across town, it's majestic and comforting. It's always in your field of vision telling you exactly where you are, like a clock, only, instead of telling time, it stops it. Instead of walking through time, you're just walking uptown or downtown.

Andy I know exactly what you mean.

Bob But standing right underneath it, we're suddenly thrown into time.

Andy Speaking of time, are you ready to go up?

Bob No.

Andy The sun is out again.

Bob We can step into the lobby.

Andy You know, I always think of Manhattan as a circle with the Empire State in the middle.

Bob Like a giant sundial.

Andy Maybe more like a dartboard. Everyone knows or wants to know how far away they are from the center and from everyone else. And whoever hits the bull's-eye gets the most points.

Bob The center is an illusion, a moving target.

Andy That's true. One year, so-and-so who's got the million-dollar house in St Tropez is it, but the next year, nobody cares because they've met someone else, who lives in a one-bedroom apartment, but has a million-dollar art collection.

Bob That's not exactly what I mean. This is a cosmic condition, not a social one. As you near the center, it retreats, like a black hole infinitely receding; but once you cross a certain threshold—what astrophysicists call the event horizon—there's no going back.

Andy The event horizon? That sounds like something social.

Bob It's not. The black hole's gravitational force draws you in until you are compressed into its infinitely dense core.

Andy Is that what happened in *2001*?

Bob No. A black hole is a rupture in the fabric of space-time. To use another example, we should be wondering what time is the time of the

Empire State? Is it human time, logical time, the time of computers? Or is it geological time? Every civilization has its own time. Christianity had the time of judgement. Today, we no longer know what time is ours.

Andy That's not true. Our time is money-time. Time is money.

Bob Money is an abstraction. What kind of time is the time of abstraction?

Andy You should invite people over and show pictures. Suddenly, everyone's got all the time in the world. In fact, that's how I met you the first time. You came to watch one of our movies.

Bob In fact, it was *Empire*.

Andy Well, that's not surprising.

Bob I watched the whole thing. That was when I first wondered if there's more than one kind of time.

Andy Really?

Bob Yes. *Empire* opened a different dimension of time. I realized that artists, by focusing so entirely on the art "object," have lost their sense of time.

Andy Really?

Bob Mostly because they're always trying to present their work to critics, collectors, or art "professionals," who believe art is either "timeless" or the product of "no time at all."

Andy I've never considered that.

Bob The Empire State wants to be "timeless," but in reality, it's a labyrinth where one loses oneself in time. Few artworks manage to achieve this, not even Judd's "specific objects" or Morris' *gestalts*. They remain trapped in a dialectic of form and presentation. The Empire State opens a dialectic of time as it really exists.

Andy What do you mean?

Bob In the real world, the only thing "timeless" is catastrophe. It maintains the world out of balance and always hints at the disasters to come. At the top of the Empire State, we're able to imagine the pre- and post-historic, where remote futures meet remote pasts.

Andy Maybe the Twin Towers aren't so bad then.

Bob How's that?

Andy One could be sort of ... you know ... the past, and the other could be the future.

Bob And in between would be the present?

Andy I guess. Anyway, two are always better than one, and then you can have sort of what you were talking about. One can be "before," and the other can be "after."

Bob The real question you have to ask about the Twin Towers is whether they're identical or whether they're the same. The difference is critical.

Andy What difference?

Bob When you have an identity, you also have reflection, which is one kind of infinity, a formal and historical one that postulates "before" and "after." In other words, you have Clement Greenberg and the avant-garde.

Andy   I don't want to have an identity, which is maybe why I don't reflect.

Bob   For example, the Quattrocento comes before the Baroque only if you know that the Quattrocento was identical to its own historical self-image and wasn't contaminated by the Romantic or the Modern. "Before" and "after" are not valid without identity; they are mapped across a pure present, so the Twin Towers as you describe them would fall in this group as well, though not the Empire State.

Andy   If the present is pure, does that mean it never goes away?

Bob   If art remains a constant through time, something that one must acknowledge if one wants to tell its history, it must always express identity. If it is merely the same throughout, then our historical timelines dissolve.

Andy   To tell you the truth, it's all the same to me.

Bob   Sameness is indifferent to historical identities. It collapses the mimetic paradigm for art and asserts the rights of time over the chronologies of history. With sameness, we're faced with another kind of infinity.

Andy   Where did you learn about all these infinities, Bob?

Bob   What I'm saying is, whatever were the actual reasons for building the Twin Towers, they were also built to stabilize the entropic force of the Empire State building. With one, sameness asserts itself too boldly. With two, they were seeking to shore up reflection.

Andy   What you're saying sounds like what you said earlier: one image needs another.

Bob   Exactly. Greenberg may have been wrong to hold onto formal notions like surface, but once the reflexive infinity of identity is mapped onto "content" rather than "form," critics and artists will once again deploy historical and political calculations of identity. He was trying to save art from excessive politicization in the 1930s, but the culture industry is demanding dollars and sense in its artistic productions.

Andy Dollars and sense?

Bob It's the only way to produce the slow shift from the Empire State to the international corporation, from the occupation of space and place to the invisible hand of the market, which is in no place and knows no space, only the geometry of dollars and sense.

Andy That makes sense to me.

Bob It's only a matter of time before relativism transforms all art into styles that succeed each other, and collapse in the same moment they triumph.

Andy But they're called *twin* towers, so maybe they're not identical and not the same. Maybe they're just ... um ... twin.

Bob There's still the question of whether the two structures make up a single thing, as they might in Judd, where you have three, four, or ten parts forming a whole. Or whether they're plural.

Andy I guess I like the idea of twins. Having a twin would make things so much easier. You could send your twin to go to all the events you have to attend but don't want to, so you could stay home and watch television. The two of you could share one life so that you could do twice the amount of work. And if there were three or four of you, just imagine what you could do.

Bob So for you, "twin" just means "more."

Andy Well, two is more than one, and three is more than two.

Bob We could visit the Twin Towers after we see the Empire State, but I don't think it'd be worth it.

Andy Why not?

Bob Visiting them doesn't mean you're brushing them against the grain.

Andy I guess not.

Bob My guess is, the view you're meant to contemplate from the Twin Towers is not really the city, the river, the bay, or anything else around it, but rather the other tower.

Andy You really think so?

Bob It's meant to deny that it's a lonely outpost at the edge of civilization and to pretend it's one of many such places, as normal as any other. The Empire State doesn't do that.

Andy I guess not.

Bob As you stand and turn in place to take in what's around you, the panorama appears not as a series of distinct, distant places, but as one unified, homogenous space, one vast world of trade, one world unified by the power of your look.

Andy But if there were two towers, aren't there two centers and two looks?

Bob The tower I would see beside me would become a substitute for every other building or skyscraper in every other city. They would cease to belong to "another world" and become part of my world, which now stretched in all directions around me.

Andy I've always thought we're all part of the same world.

Bob If that's true, the entire history of art dissolves into a diaphanous, shapeless hallucination of sameness, and history becomes a taxonomy of styles. The world loses its distances and space becomes a container rather than what separates places. East and West, Ottoman and European, North and South become just local color.

Andy Identical or same, if you ask me, it's just a matter of style.

Bob Do we really need the petty histories that have been turned out by critics who can't see past their own personal problems? The history of art can't save the concept of style because it both brings it into being and guarantees its impotence. It's a paradox that must be faced squarely rather than resolved and explained away. The more art history tries to save style through its endless proliferation, the more styles there are, the more art there is, but the more art there is, the less style becomes "just another style" or "art" no better and no worse than any other. This art or that art: when they're all equal, they're all equally impotent and worthless. Nabokov, Beckett, and Borges, to name just a few writers, recognized this danger, and sought to save literature from "literature."

Andy I didn't know you were such an elitist. I don't see why everyone shouldn't have their own art.

Bob "Art" kills art—or, rather, since art is never alive, it animates "art" monsters that devour each other. History invents continuity out of things that are discontinuous. Rescuing art from museums, collections, and art history would be the first step in freeing it from cultural confinement.

Andy That sounds like a good idea.

Bob   The Empire State is a potentially infinite expansion of a discontinuity, the eruption of a full void that doesn't distinguish styles and has no history. It liberates style form the spatial metaphor history constructs for it. The question is whether the Twin Towers also mark this space as void, or whether they fill it.

Andy   It sounds like you're about to tell me.

Bob   The Empire State articulates space by occupying the center: it takes space. But the Twin Towers mark the space between and around them: they make space. In reality, I think, they should be understood as an attempt to turn the Empire State's *sameness* into reflection. I'm even tempted to say they are architectural style in battle with itself.

Andy   Style is about everything being the same, so I don't see why you think they're battling.

Bob   True, but more so than painting or sculpture ever were, architecture is an art of imitation. In this sense, the Twin Towers are pre-historic and magical—pre-modern.

Andy   Then maybe we don't need to visit them. It seems like a lot of effort for one day. We've been standing here for a while now.

Bob   It's only from up there that you can begin to experience the leveling of the earth around you. From here, the dizzying heights throw you out of art history and into pasts and futures that are alive today.

Andy   How does it do that?

Bob   Pre-history is not what came before, but a way of feeling located in history.

Andy   You know, when we were filming *Empire*, some of the kids tried to count the floors one at a time. I couldn't make it to ten, and everyone would lose count by 30 or 40.

Bob   The Empire State is uncountable. History, on the other hand, can't stop counting: 90 stories for this building, one hundred for that one, and for the other, one hundred and one. History is less continuity than count-annuity.

Andy   What?

Bob   It earns interest on its investments in counting, just like insurance companies do.

Andy   Doesn't everyone need insurance?

Bob   It's just a figure of speech. The Empire State refuses to submit itself to the ledger-sheets of overwhelming rationalism.

Andy   What do you mean by that?

Bob   The Empire State and the World Trade Center, whatever the difference between them, are more than just points in the history of architecture. They're monuments that allow us to see the results of two thousand years of culture in the blink of an eye.

Andy   But they're so American.

Bob   They belong to the era when man builds towers into the sky for himself rather than for his gods. Instead of causing us to remember the past like old monuments, these monuments cause us to forget the future.[1]

Andy   That's interesting. I never knew you could remember it. But I guess we're still standing here and we've forgotten that we were going to go up. Do you still want to do that?

Bob In a moment.

Andy Okay, but this is the last time.

There was no one—really no one—on the street, and it was making me anxious. I suppose I was hoping that we'd find people—security guards, tourists, families, anyone—upstairs.

Bob Let's say you're standing at the top of one of the Twin Towers. You look over to the other building and someone is standing on the observation deck, and he's looking at you just like you're looking at him. The two of you are looking at each other instead of looking out on the bay, or down on the streets. Suddenly, you grow self-conscious and start to feel like a tourist.

Andy Why's that?

Bob Because you are a tourist, and what's worse, you can see yourself as one. There can be no sublime experience in that, but you realize that as a tourist on top of the world, that's precisely what you're looking for, and the minute you see yourself, you want to be different, somehow, from that other guy, standing next to you, looking for the same experience.

Andy You're probably right because I went to a party there just after they finished building them. Only one of the buildings has an observation deck, so I guess they thought of that.

Bob Unconsciously, no doubt. It would not be a satisfying touristic experience.

Andy You'd be amazed how much they pay attention to things like that.

Bob Perhaps, but in comparison the Empire State produces something very different from that kind of identification and reflection. Instead, its structure is circular and unending. It has the shape of time, and it shapes time into a circle. The Empire State is Ultramoderne.

Andy I've never heard of that, but it sounds great.

Bob The Ultramoderne buildings of the 1930s transcend Modernist "historicist" realism and naturalism, and avoid the avant-garde categories of "painting, sculpture, and architecture." The Ultraist does not "make" history in order to impress those who believe in one history. The Twin Towers, though they might seem to embrace Ultraisms's love for repetition, continue to shape space, and so they are Modernist. The distance between them is false.

Andy Did you hear about that guy who walked between them on a tightrope?

Bob I didn't, but that's only more evidence that the Towers are Modern through and through. The Empire State is neither a thing or a place. It's a sign, more like the ziggurats or the pyramids. It's like a prime number, a little gateway to infinity.

Andy I never thought about that, Bob, but it sounds like you've really put your finger on it. People are sleeping in pyramid-shaped spaces a lot now because they think it will keep them young and vital and stop the aging process.[2]

Bob What's deceptive is that it's out in the open, not buried in the deepest basement of the dustiest library, but right out where everyone can see it. Yet, because they can see it, they think they know what it is. I suppose that ultimately earthworks ought to be placed right in the middle of where we live, not in the middle of nowhere.

That's funny, I thought. I wonder what Brigid would say if I told her what Bob had just said about being "somewhere" and "nowhere."

Andy Maybe, but if you've got something that works for you, I don't know if you should stop doing it. It'll confuse people.

Bob Andy, *you've* changed careers more than once.

Andy You could see it that way. The way I see it, I always do exactly the same thing. I guess that's what I like about the Towers. They're boxy and boring like me, but that's why they're glamorous.

Bob They're more than glamorous. They're like the Pyramids and the ziggurats combined, and they've got an impassiveness that one can only associate with death. The Egyptians and the Aztecs would never have assigned so much stature to anything other than death.

Andy I guess that's true. The dead are always more glamorous.

Bob Death is absolutely glamorous. That's why the Pyramids, the prime objects, were also tombs.

Andy What do you mean by "prime objects"?

Bob No. Prime numbers, which are divisible only by themselves and one. It means they're inexpressible by anything other than themselves and the generic notion of the object itself, the number one. So a prime object is one that's untranslatable into any other form. The Great Pyramid would qualify as a prime object, even though it wouldn't qualify, for example, as a Juddian "specific object."

Andy Why not?

Bob The purpose of the Great Pyramid was defined by the Hebrews centuries ago. The name they gave it, "Urimiddon," means "Light Measures," and the Phoenicians called it "Baal-Middon," the "Lord of the Measures." In Greek, it became "Pyra-midos" or "Pyramid," a "beacon of reflections," and a "monuments of measures." As a figure of measures, it's more than just itself. It's also an image.[3]

Andy An image of the number one. Now that's really American. If Jaspers hadn't done them already, I would have done number paintings a long time ago.

Bob America is 1 equals 1.

Andy Oh, I like that.

Bob What I'm trying to say is that I don't think the Twin Towers express an identity, though they would like to. They're not two, they're a one that would like to be equal to itself.

Andy If I had to build the Empire State again, I think I'd still choose to build more than one. The idea that every building has to be different bothers me. Why can't they just find the best kind of building and stick to it? Even if it weren't all the same, then at least double: two Empire States, two Fifth Avenues, two Broadways.

Bob By that logic, they should build New York all over again, just across the river.

Andy That would be great. Then, if you want to go somewhere and it's too crowded, you just take a cab and go to the other one. That's almost as good as having a twin.

Bob You could even have both, a twin and a twin city, and the two of you could go to two of the same things. There would be no chance that you'd meet in the same place because one will go to one New York one week, and the other goes the next. You'd never get bored because you'd always be trying to figure out what the other had said and done on the other side.

Andy That would be fascinating. The next morning you could compare notes and find out who said what. It would be like you were there, but you weren't. I've always dreamed about that.

Bob was grinning. How come no one takes me seriously when I'm being serious, while whenever I'm not serious, everyone thinks I am?

Andy So, are you ready to go up now?

Bob Now I think I'm ready.

We'd come back outside, and Bob looked up one last time. For a moment, he looked like one of those old Hollywood movie stars. You know, the ones who squint when they're supposed to be acting. He looked at me and squinted, and I couldn't help thinking "you're a pretty good actor, Bob." Then we went inside and made our way to the elevators.

Andy Bob, you should be in one of my movies.

Bob You think so?

Andy Don't you want to be in the movies?

Bob It hadn't occurred to me.

Andy Everyone wants to be in a movie. At the very least you could do a screen test.

Bob I prefer to make my own.

Andy You never put anyone in them except yourself, and maybe rocks and dirt and things like that.

Bob And what's wrong with that?

Andy   People are just like crystals, rocks, and water. They look complicated, but in the end, they're not.

Bob   Isn't it the other way around? Crystals, rocks, and water are, like the Empire State, infinite structures.

When we got to the elevators, which all looked like they'd been waiting there all morning just for us, Bob slowed down, then started shuffling backward. He grew pale, sort of, and started looking as if there was something really wrong with him.

Andy   What's the matter?

Bob   Nothing. I just need a moment.

Andy   Are you edgy because we haven't seen a single person this morning? I am.

Bob   Yes, I've noticed that too, but the truth is that I've never been to the top before.

Andy   You made that pretty clear.

Bob   I have a phobia of elevators.

Andy   So when you wrote, "The arduous thoughts of the Empire State fill one with thoughts of extinguishments and vertigo," you really meant it.[4]

Don't ask me where this came from. It must have been something Brigid had been reading aloud and just got stuck in my head. How I remembered it, I really have no idea.

Bob   I have problems staying in elevators for extended periods of time.

Andy Are you trying to tell me you don't want to go up?

Bob No, no, I want to go up, but stepping into an elevator is like stepping into a time machine, so you have to give me a minute.

Andy It'll be over before you know it.

Bob I have vertigo.

Andy Didn't you fly around in a helicopter to make the jetty movie? I remember those shots. They made me dizzy. That doesn't happen with elevators.

Bob The helicopter is where this started. When the ground is so far below you, it begins to look just like a picture you'd like to make sense out of but can't. It's like flying over an image without any point of reference. It was then I started to feel like I was falling. The ground pulls away from me and dissolves, and I feel like there's nothing to hold me up.

Andy The last part of the *Spiral Jetty* is pretty abstract, but I really liked that part when you were running on the jetty to the center. When you got there, suddenly everything goes crazy. It was as if you had jumped in the water. Suddenly everything was spinning out of control. I told Paul we should try to do something like that in our next movie.

Bob It was supposed to be entropy.

Andy Is that what's happening to you now?

Bob I guess it's similar.

Andy Well, we're here now Bob, and it was your idea, so let's go because if we don't, I'll be disappointed. Just close your eyes.

I just stood there waiting for him, why I don't know. If it were anyone else, I would have pressed that "close door" button (wouldn't it be great if you could have that for everything?) and just gone up without him. But, like I said, everything was strange today, and I somehow knew that he would just get in, and I was relaxed about it. I really didn't care whether or not he got in the elevator, but I didn't care even more whether it took him two or 20 minutes. Then, after a long minute, he finally stepped into the elevator.

Andy Imagine you're in a very small apartment.

Bob I feel like I'm in a tomb and I'm being delivered to the other world.

I tried to think of something to distract him, but I think I only made it worse.

Andy I guess you've got "angst." All the Europeans always ask if I've got it.

Bob Do you?

Andy Doesn't everyone? But I'd rather be Ultraist.

Bob You mean Ultramoderne.

Andy Right.

Bob Why's that?

Andy Because it's better than Ab Ex, Minimalism, or even Pop. And it's much better than earth art, which sounds like something children do in the playground. Everything should be ultra. Is it a French word?

Bob You're thinking of "Ne plus ultra."

Andy   Right. *Ne plus ultra.* If the Empire State building is the ultra building, then maybe the World Trade Center is "ne plus ultra."

Bob   To me, it's the other way around.

When we got to the top, we walked out on the observation deck, though Bob wouldn't come anywhere near the edge.

Andy   See, that took no time at all, and it's even better than the ziggurats and the pyramids. They're just piles of rocks.

Bob   This is art after art.

Andy   See, you're feeling better already.

Bob   When a civilization builds one of these, art becomes nostalgia.

Andy   Are you sure you don't want to look down. It's really safe. You could see what it's like when you're not brushing it against the grain.

Bob   That's just a figure of speech.

Andy   It's just like all the other buildings.

Bob   It's got a sense of time all to itself. This building will outlast everything that you can see from here.

Andy   When I try to think of what time is, all I can think is: time is, time was.[5]

Bob   The Empire State is a time-figure pretending to be a space-figure. On this scale, a building no longer functions like a building. That's what I was trying to say when I presented my airport terminal project in 1967. As an aircraft ascends to higher and higher altitudes, it's meaning as an object changes—one could even say reverses. The value of the object changes as it rises higher in the sky. It's not just a building taking space.[6]

Andy It's not?

Bob It transcends the rational registers of standard meanings. This observation deck is where the Empire State ceases to be a building and becomes a pregnant instant.

Andy It's like looking at a great picture of someone famous, but not pregnant.

Bob No, it's not like looking at a picture at all. If that's what you think, why did you make your *Gold Marilyn* so small?

Andy I don't know. I guess I wanted to shrink her. You know, vertigo is a funny thing.

Bob Why is that?

Andy Because it's like being afraid of movies.

Bob I don't get that. How so?

Andy Well, I guess because being afraid of the movies means you have a fear of movement, and that's like being afraid of the ground moving below you.

Bob I'm not following you.

Andy Films are moving pictures. Maybe that's why people like photographs: because they're reassuring.

Bob That could be.

Andy   Even one of something awful or disgusting. That might sound dumb, but what do you think is the thing about a movie that you fear most?

Bob   What?

Andy   That it will end. When I watch a movie, I hope it will never end, even a really terrible movie. Which is why there are no bad, terrible movies. All movies are equal, they all move. A movie ending is kind of like hitting the ground, which is why TV is so great. You don't have to worry about it ever ending. You always know there's more tomorrow. It's like falling but knowing you won't ever hit the ground because there's no ground there to hit.

Bob   In that case, vertigo is not the fear of falling but the fear of hitting the bottom.

Andy   Sure, I guess.

Bob   I think that's where all my vertigo comes from.

Andy   I can see how you would feel that way, but I don't think you should. In fact, if you ask me, you should come over here and take a look over the edge, because that way you'll have a problem that will get rid of your problem.

Bob   Actually, I think I'm ready to go[7].

Andy   We've only been here for a few minutes. Don't you want to take in the view?

Bob   I've seen what I needed to see.

Andy   Are you sure?

Bob   I'm sure.

Imagine that I've returned from a voyage to Italy, with my imagination full of the masterpieces of ancient painting produced in that country ... As for this Italian trip which has so often been contemplated, it will never become a reality. Never, my friend, will we embrace each other in that ancient abode, silent and sacred, where men have come countless times to confess their errors or plead their needs, under this Pantheon, under these dark vaults where our souls were to have unburdened themselves ...

—Denis Diderot

Central Park

The whole way down, Bob kept his eyes closed, and all I could think of was what it would be like to do a portrait of him. Alice Neel had done a portrait of him right around the time she'd done one of me—or of one of my scars, really—so I could do a portrait of him, too. But what kind of portrait? And then it hit me: it should be a film. It should be Robert Smithson in the elevator. If I'd brought a polaroid with me, I would have snapped a few shots right there. But then nothing was normal today.

Andy Are you okay?

Bob I'm not sure.

Andy You don't look so good.

Bob Going down was worse than going up.

Andy I like going up better, too.

Most sculptors I know are pretty quiet, and I end up having to provoke them into saying something. But Bob isn't like that. When we got outside, there was still not a soul in sight. I was starting to think we'd ended up in

The Twilight Zone. There I was without a B, or with Bob as my substitute B —I guess my B's B, and I didn't know what I was going to do. I wonder if a B's B is still a B, or if there's now a C? If that's true, then the B is an A who's got his own B, and his B is really a C pretending to be a B. That would be so confusing. As far as I'm concerned, you're either an A or you're a B, and if you're not, then you're an A or a B substitute.

Bob I'll be okay. I just need some air. I don't like confinement. It starts to feel as if the whole world is compressed into a single space. I always need a little distance.

Andy There were only two of us.

Bob It's like being trapped in a movie and you can't turn away or get up and walk out but the movie is showing you nothing at all, not even motion.

Andy What are you seeing then?

Bob The nonstop stopping of motion.

Andy Speaking of movies, I was just thinking I would really like to do a film portrait of you.

Bob What did you have in mind exactly?

Andy I was sort of thinking that I could film you standing in an elevator. I know you don't like them, but it was really fascinating.

Bob I don't think that's such a good idea.

Andy To me, an elevator is an elevator. If you want, we could find a really big one, the biggest in the city.

Bob The word "elevator" is a bit sinister. It elevates us, but where to?

We usually think of elevation in lofty idealist terms, but the reality is that it imprisons us above ground, in abstractions called buildings.

Andy A lot of the time I have my best ideas when I'm in the elevator, but by the time I get out, I've forgotten them.

Bob You didn't forget it today.

Andy True. Today, I remember what I forgot I'd forgotten.

Bob Do you think people who live on high floors think they're better than others?

Andy My feeling is the higher up they are, the lower they like to go, but if they're low, then they want to go as high as they can. I knew a couple in Chicago who lived in one high-rise building and then, when a taller one was built next door, they moved into that one.[1]

Bob It used to be that people were elevated by art. Now they get that from high-rise apartments, or their suburban labyrinths situated in imaginary arcadias.

Andy Suburbs would be great if it weren't for the mosquitos.

Bob Yes, but ultimately we will have to reintegrate wilderness into the home. If we don't, we can expect innumerable films exploring the emptiness of suburbia from every possible point of view: psychological, anthropological, sociological, and metaphysical. Like the genre of the Western that preceded it, the suburban film will emerge, then slowly grow self-aware. The myth of the American outlaw will be replaced by that of the American suburbanite unable to free themselves from the laws of reason that confine him. Your films are already mapping the urban psychic landscape that will eventually become the norm.

Andy I was once in Italy for something and we were in a hotel room fourteen stories up. It was the highest I'd ever slept. Not the highest above sea level, but the highest up in a building. I always talk about how I'd love to live on the top floor of a high-rise, but when I get next to a window, I just can't handle it. I'm always afraid of rolling right out. The windows here went down so close to the floor that I'd rolled the metal shutters down the night before. I'd rather not see.[2]

Bob You seemed pretty cool with heights at the top of the Empire State.

Andy Well, we didn't have to sleep up there, did we?

Bob You always talk about how literal you are, but whenever I speak to you, I hear nothing but allegory.

Andy Really?

Bob If you're unable to look out, it's because you don't want to see how trapped you really are.

Andy Are you saying you think my fear of being up high is chemical?[1]

Bob People living high in the sky try to become the gods they once worshipped by actually putting themselves where they believe the gods once lived. But the idea that gods live high in the sky is a prejudice. The old myth of the battle of gods already tells us that the Olympians were usurpers, and the original beings, the titans, are confined deep in the bowels of the earth. Our skyscrapers only repeat the battle.

Andy For me, it's best to go neither too high nor too low. I try to hug the surface. Maybe I should buy a ranch-style house or something. I got this place out in Montauk, you know, and the house is my favorite thing, especially when I'm not there.

Bob   The home is increasingly becoming a place for transcendental longings. This will only grow worse over time as the idea of the home saps the civil and spiritual energies of America. Slowly the West will be transformed into "environments" and "habitats" for living.

Andy   What's wrong with that?

Bob   The problem is that the world is "designed" for dying. If our "homes" cannot make room for death, life will come to increasingly resemble it. Human constructions require constant surveillance in order to make sure they're "up to code."

Andy   Today, it really feels that way. What were you saying about elevators, though. You've got me confused.

Bob   Whether or not an elevator is "elevation" or not, being closed inside a metal box is not only confining, it also traps time. No matter how long one is in an elevator, it always feels like an eternity.

Andy   I think you have claustrophobia for time.

Bob   That's right.

Andy   Chronaustrophobia. Are you afraid of time or of having no time?

Bob   Chronophobia would work, but that is fear of time. Fear of the absence of time would be chronophilia.

The point of having a B, I've always thought, was to kill time.

Andy   I'm chronophobic, but I'm not claustrophobic. I have no time for time, but I have time for space.

Bob   Everyone's chronophobic because everyone's afraid of the future, or rather, the absence of a future. But to take the idea seriously, we would have to think about what exactly is the relation between time and space. What kind of spatio-temporal relation are we talking about? Is it isomorphic? Three-dimensional? Homogeneous? Infinite? Claustrophobia is obviously a little different from chronophobia but they're not unrelated. Chronaustrophobia, I would say, is the fear of time being compressed into a single moment and expanded infinitely across space.

Andy I don't know anyone who takes time seriously.

Bob That's certainly true.

Andy Are you sure you don't want me to do the portrait?

Bob I'm sure.

Andy That's fine. I'm used to not getting what I want. Especially on film. Most of the time, anyway, what's not on camera is more interesting than what is, so I spend a lot of time trying to film what I don't want so I can get what I do want.

Bob That sounds complicated.

Andy Not really. It's just a little trick you learn, just like any other trick artists figure out to get what they want.

Bob I don't think I really get what you mean.

Andy It's really not that complicated. I don't know why everyone hasn't figured this out yet. Whatever you want, you've got to not want it. And you've got to know that what you want is not what you really want, but rather the other thing that you don't want. If you want it now, it won't be the thing that you really want later.

Bob It sounds like it's a matter of timing.

Andy I guess so. You've got to not want it before so you can have what you wanted later.

Bob It's kind of a little delay you build into your process.

Andy Exactly. You know, Bob, I've filmed lots of other artists: Larry Rivers, Roy Lichtenstein, James Rosenquist. I even filmed Allen Ginsberg. He was really the best artist I ever filmed because he gave me everything that I didn't want right from the start. On the other hand, Bob Dylan came by once, but I made him wait for hours, until finally I just said no.

Bob You said no to Bob Dylan?

Andy He kept being too much of what I wanted and never became anything I didn't want.

Bob Does that mean I've got a lot of what you don't want?

Andy Sure. But not just what I don't want. You've got a lot of what other people don't want, too.

Bob What do you mean?

Andy Maybe even more than Candy Darling, who in the end has what people want even though they don't know it yet.

Bob What don't people want?

Andy Well, you're an art critic. Who wants that? Even people who read the stuff don't really want it, even though they think they want it. They don't want someone to tell them about art.

Bob Why not?

Andy Because that's what they like about art, that it doesn't tell them anything in particular. That way, they can get it to say what they want.

Bob Well, that's not exactly what I try to tell them.

Andy To tell you the truth, I was jealous for a while. I wish I could be more of what people don't want. The harder I try, the more it seems they want it. With you, they think they want it, but they really don't want it. With me, they think they don't want it, but they really do.

Bob I don't know about that. With you, it seems people get exactly what they want.

Andy You think so?

Bob In the end I don't think it matters. In geologic time, what people want or don' t want doesn' t even register in the fossil record.

Andy You see. Who'd want to hear that? I definitely do not. If only I could have filmed you saying that ...

Bob If you filmed me, here's what I would say: Ninety-ninth floor: doors, walls, lights, feeling of motion. Ninety-eighth floor: doors, walls, lights, feeling of motion. Ninety-seventh floor: doors, walls, lights, feeling of motion. Ninety-sixth floor: doors, walls, lights, feeling of motion. Ninety-fifth floor: doors, walls, lights, feeling of motion. Ninety-fourth floor: doors, walls, lights, feeling of motion. Ninety-third floor: doors, walls, lights, feeling of motion. Ninety-second floor: doors, walls, lights, feeling of motion. Ninety-first floor: doors, walls, lights, feeling of motion. Ninetieth floor: doors, walls, lights, feeling of motion ...

Andy It's good Lou Reed isn't around. He'd be so jealous.

Bob   He would?

Andy   Sure. That sounds like something he'd write.

Bob   If it were a song, I'd call it "Chronophilia." I think you've got quite a lot of it.

The other thing that you don't want with Bob is that he's always trying to convince you what he's saying is right. Who wants that?

Andy   I think I've got chronophobia.

Bob   That would be only a fear of time. Chronophilia is not only a love for time, but also a fear of its inverse: the fear of time being collapsed into space.

Andy   But I love space and I hate time.

Bob   That's not what your films say.

Andy   Well, they don't say what you say.

Bob   Let's not bicker. Museums are chronophilic. They want to extend their empires forever in the name of time, but time is one thing that always disappears when you step into a museum. Museums are spaces for the "timeless."

Andy   After five minutes, it feels like you've been there forever.

Bob   The trouble with the system nowadays is that it robs the artist of his right to his art; his time is taken from him under the pretext that his work is eternal.

Andy   Then you should just make movies. No one will ever put up with watching one in a museum.

That made him laugh. Why do people do that whenever I'm being serious?

Bob If we don't learn how to give time back to art, we will all end up in a museum, whether we make sculptures or movies. Museum directors and art historians speak openly of "institutionalization." To me, being "curated" sounds an awful lot like being "cured," don't you think?

Andy What's wrong with being cured? To be honest, I think maybe neither one of us is cured.

Bob What do you mean?

Andy Well, I didn't want to mention it, but don't you think there's something strange going on? Where is everyone?

I've never been to the desert, but this must be what it's like. Fifth Avenue was deserted. Bob wasn't really paying attention, though. He had his head craned back and was looking up at the Empire State Building again. He's a bad B.

Bob I noticed that, but I figured the street was closed for a parade or something like that.

Andy Then where are all the people, the floats, and all the cops?

Bob I don't know, but I have an idea. Why don't we walk up to Central Park? There's something there I'd like to show you.

Andy I was thinking I'd go to the office and make some phone calls.

Bob Let's just walk up to the park. You can make phone calls later.

Andy You still don't think it's a little weird that there's no one around?

Bob I do, but what can we do?

Andy You want to know what I think? I think we're dead.

Bob Well …

Andy There's really no other explanation.

Bob We could be in limbo.

Andy Is that like the *Twilight Zone*?

Bob It's where Dante put all the Greek and Latin poets, like Homer and Virgil, and the Old Testament prophets like Moses and Abraham. They weren't Christian, so they couldn't go to heaven, but he didn't want to put them in hell.

Andy So then you agree?

Bob Not really. How come then, are we the only one's here? If we're dead, we wouldn't be alone would we?

Andy Maybe when you die you just stay where you are, you can no longer see anyone who's still alive, as if someone suddenly turned off the television.

Bob Then how come we're together.

Andy I don't know. Maybe we died together.

Bob Sometimes I think that you're really a closet intellectual.

Andy Why would you say something like that?

Bob That was one of the best theories of death I've ever heard.

Andy It is?

Bob You're saying to die is to go blind to life. That's pretty good, I think.

Andy Well, it's true, don't you think?

Bob If I understand you, you're saying that death is when suddenly things are no longer far away, when they lose the minimum distance for visibility, so you can't see them anymore. You're no longer outside of the world looking at it; you've become part of it again, and therefore blind.

Andy It sounds like you think we *are* dead. Maybe Valerie Solanas really did kill me, and I've been dead for a long time and am only now realizing it. It takes a while to figure out you're alive, so maybe it's the same with figuring out you're dead.

Bob You've done a lot of work since you were shot, so I don't think you're dead.

Andy You can really get a lot done if you don't have to live.

Bob Don't be coy.

Andy You know, maybe death is when you remember everything that happens, because all of a sudden, today, I remember all sorts of things I could never remember before. In life, you forget what you do the minute you do it, but when you die, you start remembering everything you ever did second by second even though it doesn't matter anymore. That's how today feels.

Bob You're suggesting that if you were to remember everything while you're alive, then life would be just like death.

Andy Well, it's good I can't remember anything for very long—or couldn't. That's why I married my tape recorder. If I wanted to know what happened, I could just rewind. It's a lot easier that way.

Bob But then, you were trying to die even while you were—I mean are—still alive.

Andy Most people get married so they don't have to remember. When they say "till death do you part," they mean if you need to remember something, just turn to your spouse and say, "Honey, don't you remember when we were on our way to your brother's house and … " And they say "No, that was when we were visiting so and so." Married people depend on each other to remember things so neither of them can remember anything. That's how I am with my Sony.

Bob So remembering is dying, while forgetting is being alive?

Andy Sure.

Bob I just don't know.

Andy Have you noticed that even though we're walking, it doesn't feel like we're moving.

Bob Yes, I did.

We'd been heading went up Fifth Avenue, but all of a sudden we were already in front of the library.

Andy Some of the kids from the Factory used to hang around on the steps and just watch the people and the traffic go by. I remember Billy Name once telling me that it was the best movie in town because it was free, and that he'd once sat there for three days watching it. He even said he thought it was better than *Empire*. When I didn't say anything, he got nervous and thought I was angry. But I wasn't. *Empire* was only eight hours long, and I'd been thinking that maybe he was right and it should have been longer.

Bob Do you think that's why he locked himself in the darkroom?

Andy Who knows? You know, I know a way to find out if we're dead. If I call Fred or Bob and they answer the phone, then we'd know we're not dead. There's no way that they can be dead too, unless Valerie decided to kill us all. Even better, I'll call Brigid.

Bob I don't see how that would prove anything.

Andy It can't hurt.

We stopped at a phone booth and I called Brigid, but she didn't pick up. Then I tried calling Fred at home, but he wasn't there either. Where was Brigid? She never leaves the house before four or five in the afternoon.

Bob Let's not worry too much about it. Maybe it's just a coincidence.

Andy I don't know about that. Maybe if we think about what we were doing yesterday, it will make more sense.

Bob I was at home reading.

Andy What were you reading?

Bob I think it was George Kubler's *The Shape of Time*.

Andy Is that why you're so stuck on time?

Bob Maybe I'm reading the book because I'm stuck on time.

Andy I used to read, but I found someone to do it for me. It's less confusing. I used to read one book and think one thing, and then I would read another book and I'd agree with that. Now, every morning, I call up Pat—do you know her?—who is helping me write my philosophy.

Bob I didn't know you were writing another book.

Andy I'm not writing it, Pat is, her and a young guy we hired to work on the magazine. Truman Capote once told me that I reminded him of Socrates because he never wrote anything either.

Bob Socrates asked a lot of questions.

Andy I do that. Except with Pat, it's the other way around. I say, "Pat, ask me a question," and she'll ask me something, and I'll tell her what I think, and she writes it down. Sometimes she'll read something to me, usually what someone wrote or said about me, and I'll tell her what I think about it. It's much easier than reading what other people think or writing something yourself. To be honest, I don't see how anyone manages to write anything. You've got to have a good memory.

Bob You reminded me of something Kubler wrote: "Actuality is the interchronic pause when nothing is happening. It is the void between events."

Andy That's interesting.

Bob For me, writing is necessary to transcend the empty dichotomy of forms and content, all the hollow Platonisms and empty ideations of "culture."

Andy I never really got "culture." I'm probably too cheap.

Bob The word "culture" is a graveyard in which you'd find any number of dreams of achieving "culture."

Andy What do they call it when you put two ideas together that don't fit.

Bob An oxymoron.

Andy When you put money and culture together, you get an oxymoron. That's the best way to use words.

Bob An oxymoron for its own sake strikes me as very formal. Someone like Frederick Law Olmsted, who created new cultural space out of the ruins of 18th-century garden design by deformalizing it, is more interesting. He took old words like "picturesque" and recast them to make Central Park.

Andy Speaking of Central Park, if we're really dead, then I don't see why we need to go.

Bob If we're really dead, then why not go? Andy, there's something there that I think you really ought to see. Our culture has lost its sense of death, so it can kill both mentally and physically, thinking all the time that it's establishing the most creative order possible.

Andy All this talking about death reminds me of hotels. Maybe we can stop by the Pierre.

Bob What do you want to go there for?

Andy It's not very far. Who knows who'll be passing through? Did you know Robert Kennedy was killed the same day I was shot.

Bob Can I show you what I want to show you first?

Andy Sure.

Bob pointed up the avenue, which was empty and looked like one of those Renaissance paintings of places with no one in them. Except there were no columns, like there always are in those paintings. There was just building after building, window after window. Billy is right about New York being a movie. But you don't just see it from the steps of the library. You really see it walking up the avenue, or maybe it's more like one long commercial. Either way, you're living in a picture, only it stands still when you stand still and it moves when you move.

Andy Don't you love Fifth Avenue? It's my favorite.

Bob I thought Madison was your favorite.

Andy Fifth is my favorite, too.

Bob You have two favorites?

Andy Doesn't everyone?

Bob Fifth and Madison are both so much like museums. I'm surprised. I thought you didn't care for landscape, especially historical landscape.

Andy They've got the best shopping. Landscape is all about shopping: you go out on the land, you find things, and you bring them home.

Bob Well, I guess that's true, but …

Andy I did my cows, didn't I? A cow is always landscape.

Bob Yes, but it's landscape turned into wallpaper—into environment. There's another way to imagine landscape so it doesn't reflect our own desires.

Andy Oh? What does that look like?

Bob It's a landscape that's no longer anthropomorphic or even historic, but "picturesque."

Andy Is that like statuesque?

Bob A true landscape is empty. It has nothing, not even land.

Andy It's totally empty?

Bob A landscape that is not merely the projection of our desires is a region between events where nothing happens. It exists in the blank areas one never looks at.

Andy Well, usually there's not much happening in landscapes.

Bob Nothing. One could create a museum devoted to different kinds of emptiness.

Andy They've already got a few of those.

Bob Another option is the dialectical landscape.

Andy I've never seen one of those.

Bob Central Park is the best example I know. Rather than seeking to make something "timeless," a dialectic preserves the contradictory dimensions of a time and place.

Andy That also sounds a lot like abstract art, at least what they say about it.

Bob Actually, the contradiction of the picturesque departs from abstraction's static, formalist views of nature. Far from being an inner movement of the mind, it's actually based on real land and precedes the mind in its material external existence.

We arrived at Sixth Avenue and started heading up toward the park. There was a lot of construction going on: cranes, cement mixers, bulldozers, etc. All kinds of machines were sitting around idle, with no one to them work. The whole thing sort of looked like a movie set. All I could think was, "We're definitely dead."

Bob Have you ever done any other landscapes?

Andy I don't think so.

Bob Why's that?

Andy Maybe because they're about standing still, and I'm always moving, except when I'm watching TV, and then the picture is moving. If you're moving, your landscape will just be a blur, and then you'd be doing blur paintings rather than landscapes.

Bob Is that why you started to make films?

Andy Maybe, but when I think about it, I'd say that I do landscape in my own way.

Bob How so?

Andy In my business art. My style has always been to spread out, rather than move up. The ladder of success moves sideways rather than vertically. Business art is landscape art because it's about trying to spread out in a real way.

Bob So you're saying business art is a form of dialectical landscape.

Andy   Sure. In business art, you're always trying to figure out how to juggle a lot of different things, so I think it's like what you were saying.

Bob   Dialectical?

Andy   Right.

Bob   I don't know about that. In *Spiral Jetty*, I wanted to show that what comes after the one-sided idealism of Modern formalism is not just the disappearance of the work.

Andy   I remember that last shot showing the film reel spooled up on the editing table. I really liked that because it looked like a person's face but it was also a spiral. I turned to Fred and said, "Bob knows exactly how to handle shooting people: like they were just things. That's what we should do."

Bob   But that wasn't a person.

Andy   Well, you know what I mean.

Bob   The jetty is not just a sculpture. It's also a film and an article. Both are documents of its disappearance. The reel of film really isn't much more than that.

Andy   It was very glamorous, if you ask me.

Bob   A document is always an artifact of the disappearance of its object.

Andy   Sure.

Bob   Art today is slowly disappearing into categories of art.

Andy Why's that?

Bob Because European art was ripped out of total artistic structures and reclassified as painting, sculpture, and architecture. Now these categories are splintering into more and more categories.[3]

Andy That sounds a lot like what happens to me sometimes when I'm talking. I mix up my words and I start to patch.[4]

Bob Art needs to find new limits. Without them, it's lost.

Andy Sometimes I have word spasms where the parts of some words begin to sound peculiar to me and in the middle of something I'm saying, and I think "Oh, this can't be right. I don't know if I should try to finish it or say something else, because if it comes out good it'll be alright, but if it comes out bad it'll sound dumb," especially in the middle of words. Then I sometimes try to graft other words on top of them. Sometimes this makes good journalism and when they quote me it looks good in print. Other times it's very embarrassing. You can never predict what will happen when you start to patch.[5]

We came up to another construction site, where Bob suddenly stopped.

Bob It's not hard to see what will happen here.

Andy A new building.

Bob More than one. This scene will repeat itself over and over until one day Sixth Avenue will be a canyon of new monuments. From then on, we will no longer be able to distinguish between past and future. The pure present these monuments wish to be opens a passage to the prehistoric and forgets the future.[6] At that point, we will be robbed of our time, we'll feel more and more that we don't have any time.

Andy Is that good or bad?

Bob It seems tragic, but what will relieve it is irony.[7]

Andy It seems like there's not going to be any tomorrow for you or me. Just today.

Bob That's a bit morbid.

Andy I can never tell the difference between when I am and when I'm not.

Bob High seriousness and high humor are the same thing.[8]

From where I was standing, I could see the marquee of Radio City Music Hall, and I thought if ever there was a building that would always be different from the others, that was it. I remember being a kid in Pittsburgh and wondering what a radio city was, and then I thought, now's the perfect time to find out, because I'm sure Bob will tell me.

Andy What about Radio City? Do you think it has a future?

Bob The radio age is over. The voice has been swallowed by the image. Television is radio cubed. The voice speaking to us from the box was not sustainable after the war once distance was seen as a good thing. More and more, though no one can handle distance, especially in art.

Andy You can always see who's talking on TV.

Bob When television shows you someone somewhere, you're not really there, but you're no longer where you are either.

Andy I love watching someone I've met on TV, because the next time I see them, I feel like I know them better than I did before.

Bob The radio city dissolves distance, but it doesn't bring us any closer. The media substitutes a sense of closeness that doesn't safeguard its distance. That's been true since the days of the telephone.

Andy I always thought that to be close you needed to keep some distance.

Bob You're being glib.

I didn't say anything to that, so Bob pointed to the construction site down the street.

Bob The worst part is, whatever they're building makes us incapable of telling time. Everyone will be rushing around looking at their watches, but they will see it as little more than a series of instants that unfold as meetings, appointments, lunch, work, and so on. Their schedules imitate the buildings, which imitate their schedule books. But no one has a circular schedule book.

Andy I go from the moment I wake up in the morning to the time I go to bed. If I stop, I start making phone calls.

Ahead of us was Central Park.

Bob Every object, if it's art, is charged with the rush of time, even if it's static, but there will be no room for that in this future, even if every building has a plaza set aside for sculpture. [9]

Andy Well, Central Park isn't that far away.

Bob We're almost there.

Andy I usually never go into the park.

Bob Why not?

Andy I get lost.

Bob It's really not that complicated.

Andy I mean I lose all sense of which way I ought to go. On the street, I always know where I have to be and what I have to do, but there, I forget everything.

Bob Why don't you take someone with you, like you do when you go out, who'll make sure to get you where you're going?

Andy What I like about walking on the street is that the city—the buildings, the streets, the avenues, the whole skyline—becomes my B, so then I don't need anyone to go with me. Not to mention that I can always find a taxi.

Bob Well, there's no chance of that now. Plus, I'm here, so you don't have to worry.

Andy The problem is that in the park, there's too much space around me. I want to go in many directions all at the same time. I usually want more space in my life, but not that much.

Bob There really isn't anything you *ought* to do. That's why in the end, every system and philosophy collapses.

Andy But I don't have a system.

Bob You do have a philosophy, don't you?

Andy I guess, but I can't really remember what it is. Mostly if I have nothing to do, I watch television.

Bob A lot of people do that.

Andy In the park, I feel like I have to do something, but I don't know what it is.

Bob Television feels like doing nothing, but really it's listening to someone who is telling you what to do. There are better ways of doing nothing. Going to the park, for example, which really puts you in the void.

Andy People come to look at the park. That's not nothing.

Bob True. As you walk along, particular spots in the park are designed to present you with particular vistas.

Andy Sort of like television, except you can't buy them.

Bob If you learn what and where they are, you won't feel lost.

Andy Wouldn't it be great if you could do a television show from the park? Then everyone, not just the people in New York, could visit it.

Bob Like the Empire State, the park is designed for the eye as a series of pictures, all of them meant to be seen. And yet, ultimately, it's invisible. The play of the visible and the invisible is one of the basic aspects of the design.

Andy It was just an idea.

Bob One day, when all of Sixth Avenue will form two converging perspective lines, the Park will actually appear like what it already is, a vanishing point for the city grid. The park is the place where your eye gets lost, goes down a rabbit hole like Alice, and ends up in another dimension.

Andy I thought the vanishing point for the city was somewhere in space, and all the buildings were pointing to it. Isn't that what we were saying, that the city is built to go up?

Bob   No. Like we were saying about the Empire State, the vanishing point of the heavens, the infinite, is denied by the city. In its place, we have an ever-expanding space. We usually think of New York as a city that's all about verticality, but the truth is that the vertical is an ideal rather than real vanishing point, not the city as it really is, but the city as it wishes it were—a verticality in which everyone looks and finds themselves and knows where they are at all times, but only in ideal terms. That's how the city transcends space and becomes a "state of mind." The Empire State, though, is another "state of mind," a state of being "out of your mind." It transcends place, but without becoming transcendental.

Andy   You know, they have places for people who are out of their minds.

Bob   True, but just as the limit of the vertical is where the self-reflection of the city begins to corrode, so Central Park is a void space that undoes the grid—except that it's horizontal.

Andy   Are museums vertical or horizontal?

Bob   The museum, like the cathedral and the skyscraper, is a vertical institution. It displaces you, that's true, but without realizing any ideals. That is its ideal. The best thing you can say about museums is that they really are nullifying in regard to action, and that's one of their major virtues.[10]

Andy   Most are just boxy. Well, don't you think it's good to have nothing happening sometimes?

Bob   I'm interested in this sort of not-happening.[11] Central Park, though, deals not with ideals but with realities. It locates the infinite inside the city as a constitutive part of it. Circular time displaced by Sixth Avenue's linear time becomes the circularity of the park's drives, though there's nothing inherently leisurly about going in circles.

Andy That's why I get lost: I start feeling like I'm walking in circles.

Bob Olmsted gave the city a vanishing point that he knew it needed, one that's inside the city, rather than outside it, and in doing so, he gave it a limit similar to the observation deck of the Empire State. The picturesque composition of its vistas doesn't really show you anything; on the contrary, it stops the eye. Central Park is meant to be seen, but only so that it can stop the eye in its track.

Andy I guess if you want something picturesque, you should look at pictures.

Bob Unlike most pictures, Central Park has two vanishing points.

Andy More than two. I bet there's vanishing all over the place.

Bob There's the vanishing point of the image, which allows us to see three dimensions in two. There's also the vanishing point of things, which allows us to map what has three dimensions onto the fourth dimension. The eye is arrested because of its ability to throw itself, so to speak, into time.

Andy I didn't know anyone had to throw themselves into time.

Bob Time turns metaphors into things and stacks them up in cold rooms.[12] With the park, the opposite happens. Cold things are turned into metaphors.

Andy Anyone would be confused, except, I guess, critics. They love metaphors more than people or things.

Bob In Renaissance perspective, the vanishing point is a hole in the picture that organizes its surface; in the case of sculpture, a thing is a hole in a thing it is not.[13]

Andy Or maybe a thing is a thing in a hole.

Bob Let's just take the example of the landscape we have in front of us, Sixth Avenue leading up to the park. It feels almost like we're falling through time.

Andy Are you having vertigo again? We're not even in an elevator.

Bob It's almost like a memory, but of something that hasn't happened yet.

Andy What's not happened yet?

Bob The future.

Andy Oh.

Bob You're surprised?

Andy No. That's what I would say, I guess, but now it doesn't matter anymore, because we're dead.

Bob You keep saying that, almost like you wished it were true.

Andy Today I remember more than I could while I was alive, though I don't really see why I have to remember anything at all now that I'm dead.

Bob To me, it raises some interesting questions about the shape of time.

Andy That's because you were just reading about it.

Bob If time is a line, then death is always in the future. But if it's a circle, then things are more complicated.

Andy You think so?

Bob Death can only be an absence of movement, like falling to the steady side of a circle.

Andy I don't know what you mean. Why wouldn't we be back in time?

Bob It's circular, but not a circle. It's also irreversible.

Andy You're going to have to explain that.

Bob Here's a jejune experiment. Imagine a sandbox divided in half. One side has all black sand, the other side has all white sand.[14]

Andy That's easy.

Bob Take a child and have him run hundreds of times clockwise until the sand gets mixed up and begins to turn grey. After that, we have him run in the other direction. The result will not be a restoration of the original but a greater degree of greyness and an increase in entropy.[15]

Andy I see.

Bob Good.

Andy That means we can't go back and we're dead.

Bob It only means time has direction.

Andy If we filmed your experiment, we could make the sand go back to where it was by playing the film backwards.

Bob True, but eventually even the film would succumb to irreversibility and disintegrate. Why do people think film offers escape from entropy and dissolution?

Andy I guess I don't really mind. It makes things easier if we're dead. In fact, I even don't mind going into the park with you now. I would never do that if I were still alive, so I guess being dead is when you do all the things you wouldn't do in life, like walking up Sixth Avenue.

Bob So we can keep going?

Andy Sure.

Bob Good. You know, in the Renaissance they believed that perspective offered not only a proportional representation of things, but also that all earthly things were subject to the vanishing point that organized the visual field. This vanishing point was the place of the future. For Christians, that was Judgement Day, and it governed objects in the world and our vision of them. Perspective painting was equal in their minds to the judgement of the future, which saw and measured all things.

Andy From the future?

Bob Of course. It united art under the banner of a known and unavoidable future compressed into the infinitely small vanishing point. Painting—even abstract painting—always had this point. Sculpture has only discovered it recently.

Andy I never saw the point in using perspective.

Bob The vanishing point was the end of time, the invisible key that organized the visible world. Perspective was an imitation of God's judgement, which is instantaneous and immediate.

Andy Isn't that true for every artist?

Bob I suppose, but without going so far as to say that perception is learned rather than some natural gift. Because it represented a divine view of the world, perspective never needed the help of critical judgement; it actually prevented its emergence. It was only afterward that people began to feel the need to criticize art. Today, we believe perspective was a way to join vision to reason, the realm of the senses to the realm of meaning, but that's criticism projecting its own operational gestures onto an era that would not have acknowledged any identity between the human eye and the mind. Every artist that fails to learn this lesson becomes mired in the swamps of the worst kind of Romanticism.

Andy I think you're right.

Bob When they say that with perspective, reason was "in-visioned" by painting, they aren't saying that vision was elevated to the realm of reason, but rather that reason is dissolved in the material world.

Andy For some reason, what you're saying reminds me of going to church.

Bob Church?

Andy Whenever someone mentions the word judgement, I can't help thinking of the Last Supper.

Bob Oh?

Andy I first heard of it in Sunday school.

Bob And it stayed with you?

Andy I used to think about it a lot, but then I forgot about it for a long time.

Bob Is it coming back to you?

Andy Yes, only it still doesn't make much sense to me.

Bob Why not?

Andy Well, because Jesus told Judas that he's going to betray him, so it seems to me that Jesus wanted him to do it.

Bob You think so?

Andy Judas was ready to do anything for him, so when Jesus said that's what would happen, Judas went out and did exactly what Jesus said he would, because he figured if that's what Jesus said, then that's what he should do.

Bob Why would Jesus have done that?

Andy Well one thing is that it would prove that he was the son of God. Jesus got what he wanted by getting what he didn't want.

Bob I see. Is that where you got the idea you were telling me about earlier?

Andy Which one?

Bob About getting what you want by getting what you don't want?

Andy Actually, I try to get what I don't want by getting what I want.

Bob I thought it was the opposite.

Andy I might have said that, but that's not what I meant to say.

Bob It's an interesting theory. If Jesus needed Judas's betrayal to guarantee the crucifixion, I wonder if that's what da Vinci was thinking about when he did his *Last Supper*. You could say the painting is all about how the eye betrays the mind.

Andy I always think it's my mind that's betraying me.

Bob I bet it's also what Dürer was thinking in regards to perspective in *Mourning and Melancholia*.

Andy Oh, I've seen that one too.

Bob I think it shows that Dürer grew despondent about the lack of relation between his work and the divine. It's one of the sharpest reflections about the failure of reason and human attempts to envision it.

Andy I guess I never bothered with perspective, but not for those reasons. It just slows us down too much.

Bob Perspective is not necessarily slow. Once you've made your grids, it's just like a silkscreen. At any rate, you've rediscovered it in your own way. Your silkscreens are like a vanishing point spread across the entire canvas.

Andy That's interesting.

Bob There's no way to not have a vanishing point in an image. The eye has to have somewhere to travel to and rest in, the necessary limit of all art. Formalism believes that this limit is form itself, but if that were the case, then any form would do, ultimately.

Andy I've always thought that my paintings make people vanish, so doesn't that mean they have a vanishing point? And even if they do, you've still got their name. That never vanishes. That's what's so great about fame.

Bob I don't really know what you mean.

Andy It doesn't really matter.

We arrived at the park.

Bob It's not really very far from here. Let's keep going.

Andy Is it near the carousel? Paul wanted to shoot a movie there last year and brought in some 16mm screen tests of it one day.

Bob No. It's by the obelisk behind the Metropolitan Museum.

Andy We sat around watching it, and I started to get dizzy. So I said to him, "Paul, no one got dizzy watching *Empire* or *The Chelsea Girls*." I was still thinking about what Bob had said about perspective in painting. I kept replaying different parts of it in my mind, even though normally I can't remember anything anyone says without my Sony. What did Bob mean by the "limit" of art? I decided we must be dead because I never think about that kind of thing. So maybe death is when you have all the time in the world to think. Nothing but time to think about time.

Andy If I'd been a Renaissance painter, I would have been the first in line for the grid system.

Bob Da Vinci used it. He liked machines, and the grid is just another sort of machine.

Andy Once you get a machine to go, it goes forever. Once you've invented something, you can't uninvent it. I mean, they can't uninvent the atom bomb can they?

Bob What are you trying to say?

Andy I guess that all my works have vanishing points, except that I do it a little differently than they used to in the Renaissance.

Bob How so?

Andy For me, the whole painting is a vanishing point.

Bob When I was still trying to paint, perspective was just a technical thing, so I never had much interest in doing it. What I was really looking for was a "vanishing point" for sculpture.

Andy If only sculpture could learn how to vanish.

We walked into the park. Most people think nature is where there's the fewest number of people and the greatest number of animals, but I've always felt most natural where there're a lot of people. There was no one here, and it felt so artificial, a little like we were walking through a movie set.

Andy I think I've always preferred French gardens. There you know exactly what's what.

Bob Olmsted designed the park so that the farther north you go, the more rural it begins to look. In fact, though, it's more like there are more and more images of the country. The whole thing unfolds like a series of photographs that, instead of giving it a unity of space and time, form a temporal landscape. The farther north you go, the farther back in time you're meant to travel.

Andy We're going backward in time.

Bob Not literally.

Andy Well, I wouldn't mind.

We were already walking up to the obelisk, which is just behind the Metropolitan. I remember once asking Henry Geldzahler whether he could see it from his office and he told me it didn't have a window, and that he rarely ever saw the park because he was always leaving the museum on his way to visit collectors in their apartments on the East side and never on the West Side, in which case, he would take the opportunity to walk across the park. I remember exactly what I said to him: "I guess working at the Met is like being buried in art." A few days later, though, I realized that he was lying and that he probably went to the West Side all the time. It was his little way of being nice, since he knew that East Side people liked Pop art, and West Side people liked abstraction and Minimalism and that sort of thing.

Bob You see that?

Bob pointed to a spot beside a tree not far from the obelisk.

Andy What are you pointing at?

Bob That's where Claes Oldenburg buried his cube in 1967.

Andy He buried a cube?

Bob Yes.

Andy Why?

Bob I guess he thought he was burying Modern art.

Andy I would have given it to the Museum of Modern Art. They could have buried it for him. Was it just a plain cube?

Bob A cube is a cube is a cube.

Andy There's nothing to mark the spot. Are you sure it's here and not over there? I pointed to the other side of the tree.

Bob For all its insistence on the visible and on surface, on motion, action, and movement, paint and materiality, Modernism has always been in love with the invisible. Elevating matter to the height of the ideal doesn't get us out of idealism. True abstraction would be the inverse: instead of elevation, we'd have devolution.

Andy Well, didn't we already discuss going up and going down? We don't have to talk about it again.

Bob Abstraction is not governed by "expression," or what Greenberg calls "experience," but by a mental attitude toward aesthetics that in no way depends on formal reduction. An Egyptian idol is more abstract than a Noland painting, because it excludes emotional needs. Abstract art does not appeal to the emotions but to the mind. All expressive art is representational.[16]

Andy I've always thought attitude is important.

Bob Even the Minimalists who denounced it the loudest, in spite of all the noise they make about the object, the thing, the *Gestalt* and so on, despite all the war drums against Greenberg and the painters, even they, in the end, esteem not the individual thing but the space in-between one thing and another, real, ideal, or what have you. They haven't really come to terms with theater. In that respect, the Conceptual artists drew the right conclusions from Minimalism by insisting on the problem of intention. No matter how much you talk about the object, if you've made it, found it, or destroyed it, it's an intentional thing, and every critic will begin with the idea that the object is intended to be art. There's no other way.

Andy People are always complaining that Minimalism is boring. I think it's even more boring than they realize, but that's why I like it.

Bob The minimum in Minimalism is the intention to be an object, so it's not ultimately a form of abstraction, but a desire to be present. As Worringer pointed out, any will toward space is not an abstract concern.[17]

Andy I always want more space, too.

Bob In the *Cows* and the *Silver Clouds* exhibitions, you took on what Greenberg would like to address when he talks about the "framing support" and the "picture support," but without treating it just as space, space, and more space.[18]

Andy The more space the better, but I'm not sure that a lot of space in your art is the best thing. In my art, I always fill up my spaces, though I never fill it up with just, you know, abstract stuff.

Bob The framing support has nothing to do with abstraction.[19] You blurred the relation between the frame and what's in the frame, but you didn't identify the gallery as an abstract space.

Andy A lot of people were already doing that, so I really didn't see the point.

Bob But I think that's where your vanishing point was, the invisible support. It was this invisible determiner that you exhibited in those exhibitions.

Andy But I just wanted to do cows. I didn't want to present something invisible.

Bob Then your system works. You got what you didn't want.

Andy I guess that's true.

Bob What I like about Oldenburg's work is that in burying the cube

—the generic form of space—he acknowledges the anthropomorphism of space and demolishes it at the same time.

Andy But there's nothing to see.

Bob That's true, it was a mistake to bury it completely. I would have only buried it partially.

Andy What would that do?

Bob It would let the viewer perceive the cross-section of time, but mostly it would negate the pathos of "life and death." Abstraction is not about that. On the other hand, there is no escaping nature through abstract representation; abstraction brings one close to physical structures within nature itself. But this doesn't mean we should have a renewed confidence in nature. Abstraction is no cause for faith. It can only be valid if it accepts nature's dialectic.[20] In completely burying it, Oldenburg remained in some ways a formalist.

Andy Didn't someone say you kill what you love? Only maybe he buried it before it was dead.

Bob I wouldn't use that metaphor, but I get your meaning.

Andy Speaking of death, do you think that since we're dead now, we've been buried somewhere?

Bob You really are very morbid.

Andy Have you ever thought about what they'll do with your body? I have, but I can't make up my mind. It's not like there are a lot of options. I've never liked the idea that they'll put it in the ground. The worst thing that could happen to you when you die is that you would be to be embalmed and laid up in a pyramid. I'm repulsed when I think about the

Egyptians taking each organ and embalming it separately in its own receptacle. I want my machinery to disappear.[21] Maybe I could have a mausoleum built or something like that. Then, even when you're gone, there's something left over.

Bob Oldenburg turned Central Park into modernism's crypt, but it may have already been that from the very beginning. I once buried something, but not all the way.

Andy A cube?

Bob It was called *Partially Buried Woodshed* and it was built on the campus of Kent State.

Andy I've heard of that place.

Bob The step beyond formalism has to preserve a memory of erasure.

It was then that I spotted what looked like a little shack tucked up in the side of a little rocky hill on the far end of the field. It took me a moment to see that it really was a cabin because it was camouflaged. I started to think what it would be like to make art that's camouflaged.

Andy Bob, look over there.

Bob Where?

Andy Against the hillside. It looks like there's some kind of door.

Bob I see it.

Andy It's almost like a woodshed. Did you build that?

Bob No.

Andy Well, do you think it's open?

Bob You're saying you want to take a look?

Andy Maybe just for a minute, just to get out of the sun.

Bob Alright.

The creative in photography is its capitulation to fashion. The world is beautiful—that is its watchword. In it is unmasked the posture of a photography that can endow any soup can with cosmic significance but cannot grasp a single one of the human connections in which it exists, even when this photography's most dream-laden subjects are a forerunner more of its saleability than of any knowledge it might produce.

—Walter Benjamin

Underground Cinema

Inside it was pitch black.

Bob Here we are.

Andy Is there a light?

Bob There are gaps and cracks in the wall. Your eyes will adjust in a minute.

Andy I need to know where I am. If I can't see where I am, I get nervous.

Bob Seeing never helps you know anything, especially where you are. You in particular should know that.

Andy Is that how I behaved when you were losing it in the elevator? Besides, aren't you curious to know what's in here?

Bob I doubt there's anything worth seeing.

Andy You know what I think. I think you invented that whole Oldenburg story so that you get me to come here.

Bob That's not true.

Andy Then how do you know there's nothing here to see?

Bob Okay, I admit it. I've been here before—a long time ago. But the Oldenburg cube is real. I didn't make that up.

Andy Why didn't you just say you wanted to come here?

Bob Andy, I could barely convince you to come into the park.

Andy So where are we?

Bob I think it used to be a bathroom. If you crouch down and feel the floor, it's tile. But everything was taken out or stolen a long time ago. It's quite empty.

Andy Are there others?

Bob A few. I went looking for them once I found this one, which I really found by accident. You couldn't see the door unless you peeled off several layers of ivy. The lock was rusted through. If there were others, they were closed up and sealed.

Andy I didn't think you were that adventurous.

Bob Can you see better now?

Andy Not really.

Bob I can already make out the shadows of my hands.

Andy Don't you keep a flashlight in here, or something? An artist should be prepared for anything.

Bob I didn't think you were the type to be afraid of the dark.

Andy I usually like the dark, as long as I know where I am and what's around me.

Bob Next time I'll bring one.

Andy If you ask me, there's only one real explanation for all this.

Bob What's that?

Andy It means we're really dead.

Bob How can you be sure?

Andy Weren't we just on top of the Empire State Building? We went up, then we went down. Now, we're underground. Going up turns out to be going down.

Bob Your uptown kids like to come downtown, and your down-and-outs are on their way up. It's dialectical.

Andy Would you please stop using that word.

Bob Fine, but it changes nothing.

Andy Thanks. Well, this is different from going uptown and downtown. This is creepy. I think we're being slowly buried alive.

Bob Oh don't be so lurid. Many other explanations are possible.

Andy Like what?

Bob Going underground doesn't only mean being dead. It can mean many things. You should know, you've spent a lot of time in the underground film scene.

Andy When people describe who I am—or was, I guess—if they don't say "Andy Warhol the Pop artist," they say, "Andy Warhol the underground filmmaker." Or at least they used to. But I don't even know what the term "underground" means, unless it means that you don't want anyone to find out about you or bother you. But if that's the case, I can't see how I was ever "underground," since I've always wanted people to notice me. I think Jonas Mekas once told me that it was Manny Farber who first used the word.

Bob That sounds right.

Andy He also told me that Duchamp gave a speech at some Philadelphia opening and said that the only way artists could create anything significant today was "to go underground."[1]

Bob And do you agree?

Andy Like I said, I don't know what the term means. In general, I don't worry about that sort of thing. What's possible and what's impossible is too abstract for me.

Bob You ought to.

Andy Why?

Bob For one thing, you might find yourself underground someday.

Andy Like today for instance. But I don't see how knowing what "underground" means helps us. Do you know what it means?

Bob My sense of Duchamp is that he was dissatisfied with painting and high art, so he saw any way out of art as worth a shot. His whole involvement with da Vinci seems like it was an attempt to transcend an artist with a very mechanistic view of nature, even though he himself was just as mechanistic. At least da Vinci offered something pragmatic and useful.[2]

Andy I met him once in 1962. It was at his opening at the Pasadena Museum. He was very polite. That's more than you could say for Johns and Rauschenberg. They've never come to a single one of my openings, even though I always have the kids handwrite nice invitations to them.

Bob Maybe they're jealous.

Andy Mechanistic or not, I think Duchamp would have come.

Bob I met him once in 1963 at the Cordier-Ekstrom gallery.

Andy Did you talk to him?

Bob I just said one thing: "I see you are into alchemy." And he said, "Yes."[3]

Andy I think you and Duchamp have a lot in common. The rocks, crystals, salt, and all that stuff, isn't that all about alchemy?

Bob I can't accept Duchamp. There's a huge difference between his mechanistic view and a dialectical view. His objects are just like relics of saints. He seems like he was into a kind of spiritualism of the commonplace. He was a spiritualist of Woolworth, you might say, and even if he wasn't, I'm just not interested in the occult.[4]

Andy I never understand anything about the occult, but then I think that nobody else does either. You know, Fred once told me that artists who are similar always act like two hookers on the same corner.

Bob That's a little mean. In any case, occult systems are dream world fantasties, fiction at best. At worst, they're uninteresting.[5]

Andy Don't you read a lot of science fiction? I remember you talking about it once. But I didn't know what you were talking about.

Bob Sure, but science fiction is different from fantasy.

Andy I've never really been into that sort of thing, but there doesn't seem like there's such a big difference.

Bob Fantasy is entirely disconnected from reality; science fiction, on the other hand, imagines either the unrealized possibilities of reality or its real impossibilities, whether they are scientific, social, or philosophical.

Andy That's fascinating. Do you think there's any way it could tell us what's happened and where we are?

Bob Maybe we've fallen into some kind of cryosphere.

Andy Into what?

Bob The cryosphere was a piece I showed back in 1966 in the *Primary Structures* show at the Jewish Museum. It was based on ice crystals in a hexagonal lattice set-up, which move in a kind of ambiguous flux. I like unstable materials. Gas, too, is sort of a fascinating thing.[6]

Andy That's what I've always thought.

Bob What I'm trying to say is maybe we're in some kind of ambiguous flux. Maybe what happens when you die is that you become like water or gas, always in motion. In that case, being alive would mean being fixed in place, like a solid. It may be ultimately about how much motion our molecules are permitted. Once the level of motion rises beyond a certain point, then we experience death, but really, it's more like a dispersion.

Andy   Brigid was right about you after all. You really are the "nowhere man." Or maybe you're "nowhere" and I'm "somewhere" and we're somewhere in-between.

Bob   Maybe we're both somewhere in-between solid and gas.

Andy   Wouldn't that make you feel claustrophobic?

Bob   Perhaps.

Andy   To be honest, to me it feels like we're in an Antonioni movie, only without any pretties or parties or Italian decor. Maybe *Red Desert*. It doesn't matter too much which one. In most of Antonioni's movies, the actors wander around wondering where they are and what's happening to them and why they're not happy even though they look great and have everything they ever wanted. The only difference is that we don't look so great.

Bob   Being in a movie is what life would be like not when people die, but when the whole world was converted into television, when everything was televised for everyone everywhere. That was Dziga Vertov's dream.

Andy   Whose?

Bob   One of the early Russian Futurist filmmakers who made the famous *The Man with a Movie Camera*. He tried to imagine how the new revolutionary society would be anchored on the movie camera. Whoever you were and whatever you did—whether you were a factory worker, a bus driver, a coal miner, or a magician—the cameraman would seek you out and film you at work so that you could become part of the social movie of the proletariat.

Andy You know, I've wanted to have a television show for a long time. It would be even better than making movies.

Bob Vertov imagined the camera as an instrument of the proletariat's self-actualization. He believed that if you could actually see how you fit into society as a whole, it would help you understand your role in the giant machinery of the new State. Film would be *the* art form of society because it would bring together vision and understanding.

Andy You don't need a movie camera for that.

Bob Modernism always sought to combine the two, even when it did violence to one through the other.

Andy Did he really need film? Don't you think photography is better for that kind of thing?

Bob Why is that?

Andy Well, if it weren't, newspapers would have gone out of business a long time ago, while newsreels would have made tons of money and we would see them everywhere. But we don't.

Bob Good point. Only it did happen, but it came to be called television news instead of newsreels.

Andy I didn't think of that, but I guess you're right.

Bob Television was a futurist idea. If you could see yourself at the actual moment of the present, you could control and envision the future, and propel yourself into it. It was also the way in which everyone came to see how they could be like everyone else. No matter what you did for a living, the camera could film you doing it. In Russia, the worker was the star; in the US, it's the actor, or anyone who seems to possess any sort of presence, or even, or a generic form of it.

That sounded a lot like what I'd been thinking about—how they choose people to put on the covers of magazines. You have to be weird, but you can only be weird in the way they can understand, otherwise they won't go for it. I learned that when I came to New York.

Andy Somebody told me once that Brecht wanted everybody to think alike. I want everybody to think alike too. Only, I don't like to film people at work because I think that's boring.

Bob Then how do you film them?

Andy I prefer when they don't do much, when they're just being themselves. I guess you could say I'm a futurist, but only on weekends.

Bob For Vertov, man became a machine and the machine became the art form by which the machine-man discovered himself as the machine that he was. He became a machine that could see itself; and the camera was the machine that allowed him to do this.

Andy Say that again.

Bob We ought to consider the following conundrum: a machine needs another machine to know that it's a machine; once it has seen that it's a machine, it knows that it's not human. Yet if it needs another machine to know this, doesn't that mean it's not just a machine? You would think that it's totally self-sufficient. And how does it know whether the second machine is a machine? How can it be certain the other is a machine too?

Andy The machine needs another machine to see that it's a machine.

Bob Right. Every machine needs another machine, but it needs to know that it's a machine before it can say whether the other is a machine? And it needs to know the other is a machine to know that it's a machine.

Andy Now I know why whenever you buy a gadget, they always make you buy five others to go with it, and then, a week later, you've got to buy five more. But that's probably why people need other people.

Bob Why?

Andy Because they're really machines.

Bob Well, the way I would put it is that mind needs matter, but matter doesn't need mind. It's not a symbiotic relation.

Andy I guess not. Do you know if Jonas Mekas ever showed Vertov's films at the filmmaker's coop?

Bob I think so.

Andy I think I would have seen them then, but I guess I forget everything. Or I used to.

Bob Maybe you just missed it.

Andy Maybe.

Bob I don't think we've transcended Futurism yet. We are still operating by its principles. Most art today believes in motion rather than stasis, and that was a proposition first floated by Marinetti, when he proclaimed speed, nothing but an abstract relation between motion and space, as the privileged aesthetic paradigm. Historically, it flowered into many different art styles and movements: Futurism in Italy, Cubism and abstraction first in France, then America; even the trajectory from Duchamp's *Nude Descending a Staircase* to Conceptualism. Duchamp's answer to its mechanistic and deterministic implications was to invert it —which is, as I said, equally mechanistic. Conceptualism just translated the dynamism into the frictionless motion of ideas, which is why it ends up feeling so static, the real proof that Duchamp's alchemy doesn't hold the object under the spell of the artist.

Andy Do you think, Judd, Serra, LeWitt and all those sculptor types you like to hang out with are also Futurists?

Bob Minimalism amalgamated abstraction and the readymade, but it didn't go far enough. It never questioned the historical origins of either tradition in Futurism and its mechanistic machine-ethos. What remains to be considered is a dialectical inversion.

Andy I'm starting to regret that I said I want to be a machine. It was just something to say. I was just trying to go with the flow, and it seems like everyone wants to be a Futurist machine.

Bob For Vertov, fame was the glue that held together the new society through the cinematic mechanism. Everyone was famous to everyone else via the power of the all-seeing camera eye.

Andy That sounds a lot like television.

Bob You think so?

Andy America is turning out to be more like a Communist Russia than Communist Russia. If it turns out that we're not really dead and I someday get my own television show, I'm going to call it *Nothing Special*.[7]

Bob Why's that?

Andy Because everyone on television is always saying they're the most special this and the most special that, when in fact they're really all pretty much the same.

Bob Like Eisenstein, Vertov saw the camera as less important than the film editor, who composed the image of the proletariat by literally collecting and then selecting pieces of film. In other words, even Vertov, the most idealistic of all the Russian filmmakers, acknowledged that selection was a social principle out of sheer necessity. No art form can do without it. The social *Gesamtkunstwerk* is just as much a fiction as any other film. What you're saying—and I agree with you—is that television says we're all the same even as it is itself a highly selective process that implies we're not all the same.

Andy Like a curator who puts together an exhibition.

Bob Or like a critic choosing what they will value or devalue as they conceive their historical fables. One day, television will usurp the roles of critic and curator, and in many ways the label "television producer" is the most honest one for these sorts of people. Most curators and critics act in fact more like Hollywood showmen than thinkers: their primary concern is to enforce and oversee artistic production and deliver it quickly and cheaply to its destination, as if it were a branch of the national economy.

Andy They're always complaining about money.

Bob Museum catalogs and magazine articles increasingly imitate, consciously or not, the metrics of the dismal science.

Andy If I were a curator, I would just make my own television station.

Bob Do you think you could have shown your *Mao*s on TV?

Andy Sure.

Bob How could anyone get a sense of their actual scale?

Andy Oh, that's easy. If I were a young artist starting out today, I'd make all my work in video. That way, it would already be ready for TV, and all you'd have to do to send it on its way would be to press a button. Someday, everyone will make their own art and send it to whomever they want.

Bob But Andy, putting something on TV is like embalming it. Nothing ever ages or dies. TV is timeless.

Andy Exactly my point. That's why if I were a curator, I'd definitely stop worrying about whether I could have my show in this museum or that museum. If someone wanted to look at art, they could just turn to the museum channel.

Bob Both are voids waiting to be filled. Museums fill real space, while television fills time-space.

Andy If you wanted to, you could study every inch of every painting, like the close-ups of small animals on those nature shows. Once I start watching one, I can't turn it off until one animal eats the other. Or gets sick and dies. Those are the saddest shows on TV.

Bob In pictorial terms, television is always a portrait. The portrait brings things close, but the landscape maintains a distance.

Andy You know, if I were a critic, I'd do the same thing. Why bother to write about a show, when you can just show it.

Bob I don't agree. Criticism doesn't just show art. It shows how to see it.

Andy Then why are they always putting pictures of the art right next to the article in the magazine?

Bob If I were the editor of an art magazine, there would be no images. Art writing is already guilty of acting as if it were television, bringing what is far away close. Instead, I would worry about how to preserve the distance between language and things. So long as art writing is just describing, it hasn't yet said anything, a disservice that artists should take as an insult.

Andy Most artists get upset when a review stops talking about what their work looks like—even if the critic writes nothing but good things. But I don't. I'm happy that not everyone likes the work. I've found that there's nothing worse for your values than when everyone agrees.

Bob When everyone is agreeing, people start to worry that they're just like everyone else.

Andy Bob, would you mind if I asked you a question?

Bob Not at all.

Andy Do you think I'm a communist?

Bob A communist? Why? Because you did those *Maos*?

Andy Well, the *Maos*, and the *Hammer and Sickle* paintings, too. Have you seen those? They're pretty new. But mostly because I like television and I want everyone to be the same.

Bob Is that why you started *Interview*?

Andy It's possible.

Bob I think a lot of people would say that wanting everyone to be the same means you're a communist. But I don't.

Andy To tell you the truth, I don't really see why people get so worked up about politics. I don't see how it's any different from just regular everyday socializing. It seems like politics is about everyone, so if everyone were the same, politics would be pretty easy.

Bob If everyone were the same, there wouldn't be any politics. If you're going to have a magazine about celebrities, that's not about making everyone the same. Celebrities are celebrities because they're different. But that's what we were talking about before isn't it?

Andy I don't think fame could ever be for everyone. Everyone can be famous, but not all at the same time. If that happened, then fame would stop being fame. It would just be politics, and then it would be just about different cliques fighting with each other for the most attention. I hate that kind of thing. That's been going on at the Factory for years now, and it's so tiring just trying to keep everyone happy.

Bob You're saying fame and politics are mutually exclusive?

Andy Um … I guess. Which is why, I guess, I'm not a communist. I prefer fame to politics.

Bob I think you put your finger on one of the reasons for the failure of Vertov's utopian ideas—or, rather, their success, which necessarily implies the failure of Modernism in art. The revolution was forced to find its representation not in the simultaneous fame of every single individual, which could never be accomplished, but in the individuality of the leader. Hitler, Mussolini, and even Mao. The leader is a substitute for the impossible simultaneity necessary to form an image of the desired results. The notion of "results" in Vertov has to be re-examined. The Minimalists understood this perhaps better than anyone. The simultaneity demanded by Vertov was staged by Judd and Morris, then attacked by Michael Fried as theatricality. Technically, Fried is right, but he misses the point. Every refutation is a mirror of the thing it refutes—*ad infinitum*. He dreads "distance" because that would force him to become aware of the role he is playing.[8]

Andy What you're saying happened a lot in the 1960s. People would say down with this or down with that, but the following week they would be doing exactly what they had been screaming about. It was back then that fame really got going. When you went to a party, everybody was interested in everybody else. In the 1970s, everybody started dropping everyone else. The 1960s were clutter. The 1970s are very empty. Maybe that's why I started *Interview*, to fill up all that emptiness.[9]

Bob Why didn't you consider leaving it empty?

Andy There's always more emptiness than you can fill.

Bob I suppose. Can I ask you a question now?

Andy Sure.

Bob Why Mao?

Andy Well, we were just doing films, which was fine, but then Fred said he thought we could make a lot of money in the portrait business, or maybe it was Bruno Bischofberger who suggested the idea. I can't remember.

Bob No, I mean why did you choose Mao, and not someone else?

Andy Someone came up with the idea of doing a portrait of the most important person of the 20th century, and they spent all this time trying to figure out who that was. But I thought the most important person would have to be the most famous, and they figured out that that was Mao.

Bob It's true. Mao is the greatest ideal of the Chinese masses, a dream of simultaneity.

Andy He's got a certain aura, you know.

Bob An aura? What do you mean by that?

Andy I mean, you know, when you see someone on the street who's really got something, they've got aura, at least until they open their mouths. Then, most of the time, there goes the aura.[10]

Bob But Mao is known for the things he said.

Andy Maybe, but people who know what he said probably don't feel his aura. To keep someone's aura, you've got to freeze them. So when we were trying to figure out what kind of picture to use, I made sure that he had his mouth closed and decided to have him doing nothing, not even smile. Someone with aura always stirs up a room just by being who they are, so Mao is just being himself. But there are people who have aura by opening their mouths. That's how Truman Capote is, and that's how you are, I think, Bob. Both of you have got oral aura.

Bob Are you trying to flatter me?

Andy I don't know. But like I was telling you before, Brigid likes to read your articles aloud, and she doesn't do that with any other critic, so I figure that means your words have aura.

Bob Greenberg always made sure his words were in the right place at the right time and that the right place and time were always in his words, while Judd writes a descriptive criticism full of holes.[11] Then there's LeWitt and Reinhardt and their paradoxes and histories of non-sense.[12]

Andy And you?

Bob For me, writing is moving words from one place to another.

Andy You mean like what you do with rocks and dirt?

Bob   I suppose. My writing isn't meant to exist on its own as an independent, formal work of art.

Andy So it's not really "criticism"? Because I think that's what critics often wish—that an artist's work would go away so their writing could be framed. Do you think it would make them happy if someone framed their articles?

Bob   Framing it would just turn it into an object. My writing is not a story or poetry, nor even "prose poetry." These are formal categories. Instead, I try to derealize words by layering them—like geological strata. They pile up instead like so many mountains of letters.[13]

Andy Like printed matter. That's just what we do. We have a stack of art magazines that just keeps getting bigger and bigger.

Bob   I write about art, but I don't "review" it. The implication of "second-sight" in the word "review" needs to be questioned. All writing is second-sight, but for that reason it's blind. The fictional betrays it's privileged position when it abdicates to a mindless "realism."[14]

Andy I agree one hundred percent. When we did our novel, we just recorded what everyone said, but then when we read it, it sounded like we'd made it all up. Did you know that Mao wrote poetry?

Bob Marx, too. And everyone knows the painter.

Andy It really is a little weird, I think.

Bob At the least, it suggests an affinity between the operations of art and the art of politics, though any art that tries to be political is a contradiction in terms.

Andy I think so too. I did a political poster a few years ago and it seems like it backfired.

Bob I didn't know you were interested in politics.

Andy The McGovern people had me do a poster, so we did a poster of Richard Nixon that was stamped "Vote McGovern." Nixon won. I guess people read the first word, "Vote" and then got lazy and just looked at the picture. And then Nixon had us audited. After that, I learned never to do political art, even if it's good business.

Bob All art questions what value is, but this leads to many categories of value that get mixed together to make values go up or down; for instance, political art, or art politics. The categories of "good art" and "bad art" belong to a commodity value system.[15]

Andy The way you just said that made it sound like poetry. I guess that's because Marx was a poet. I started as an illustrator, so that's why people say what I do is still like the blotted line technique I got my first jobs with. I guess he never escaped his past, but why would he want to, if it worked?

Bob No value or image is ever just there. It's always suspended in a relation with something else, something not there. Between the two lies an interval that represses the temporal dimension or quantifies it so the relation between past and future becomes like the relation between the word and its meaning.

Andy For example?

Bob Fashion. Fashion binds past and future into aura. It says, "I am different from what was yesterday and what will be tomorrow. I am today, and if you wear me, you will be present here today, and everyone will notice that you are here today, not gone like yesterday." Mao is a movie star in China because in China there's not much difference between the government and the movies.

Andy Fashion wants us to wear the same clothes everyone else does, just like Mao wanted. One day glamorous people will wear uniforms.

Bob   Soon it won't be that different here, which is probably another reason why political art is madness. Not only can no artist afford the kind of money they spend on movies in Hollywood, individual power is undermined by vague ideas like "entertainment," "culture," "education," and "sport."[16] Each of these is a specific scene in *The Man with a Movie Camera*. But speaking of movies yours have changed in the past few years.

Andy   Mostly they're not as long as they used to be.

Bob   They're not just longer or shorter. They have a different sense of time now than they used to.

Andy   Well, I guess we wasted a lot of time in the Factory watching those films. But I never regretted it. I like anything that makes time go faster.

Bob   When you abandoned montage, you opened a pure interval, a pure duration no longer mapped onto space, no longer part of the arsenal of expression. At the same time, you knocked the feet out from under structural film and that sort of thing. But I'm not clear on what you're doing now with all the stories you're writing.

Andy   Well, *Empire* had a beginning, middle, and an end. We're still doing that.

Bob   Everyone says that *Empire* was a painting, but I always thought of it more as a play. This drama threatened Michael Fried's "presentness" with the terrors of infinity, which dissolves the art-historical belief in temporal histories, empires, revolutions, and counter-revolutions. In it everything became ephemeral and unreal.[17]

Andy   We weren't trying to make a realist film, but we weren't really trying to be surreal, if you know what I mean.

Bob How did the decision to not edit happen?

Andy I don't think anyone decided. None of us really knew how to do it, mostly because no one could be bothered with keeping track of all that film. It was hard enough to keep track of who was coming and going and all the work we had to do. You know there was always a lot of stuff going on, and I could never decide what I should film, so I decided to film all of it, or as much as we could. I thought: why not let the camera do all the work? I mean, wasn't that why machines were invented, so we could get more work done and do less? Editing is so tiresome and time-consuming. So I put the camera on a tripod and turned it on. Once everything is on television, that's how everything will be, anyway.

Bob If you're right, then leisure will be the greatest kind of television. The figure of the artist emerged in the romantic period, but in the end, the artist puts himself out of work. Even if the camera were never invented, every worker, in believing in the myth of self-expression, will come to think that they, too, are artists. Vertov never considered this in his film, either, though Marinetti seemed to think it was inevitable.

Andy I guess so.

Bob In past eras, the artist was a name for an atelier that made everything form vanity portraits to architecture. The fact that we still believe in the artist, but only within the narrow confines of the gallery and the museum, only proves the obsolescence of the concept.[18]

Andy That's what I've always thought. I let the camera do what it does and let the kids be who they were. Jackie, Ondine, Mary, Edie, Ultraviolet, and all the others kept trying to act. I would tell them to stop trying so hard, but they were never happy with that. They always wanted to do something, to be glamorous and improvise, and I never understood why, because we were just trying to have some fun. But it somehow all worked out, and we ended up with a lot of film.

Bob A camera is wild in just about anybody's hands. Some artists are insane enough to imagine they can tame the wilderness created by the camera, so you have to set limits.[19]

Andy That's why I put it on a tripod.

Bob Cameras care nothing about cults or isms. They're indifferent mechanical eyes, ready to devour anything in sight. They're lenses of unlimited reproduction, machines of infinity. Like mirrors they may be scorned for their power to duplicate our individual experiences, but it's not hard to imagine an Infinite Camera without an ego.[20]

Andy That's my favorite thing about cameras. No ego. They just work and work. That's why we ended up with so much film.

Bob I remember you were screening things all the time.

Andy That's how we ended up with *Chelsea Girls*. We had all this film and we didn't know what to do with it, so I thought why not let the projectionist decide.

Bob And why did you choose to have two frames?

Andy It was so we could cut the screening time in half. We had six hours of film, but only three hours to show it.

Bob So in *Chelsea Girls* you doubled the film rather than cutting it, as montage would do.

Andy I guess.

Bob In being doubled, it was de-differentiated, separate but the same, rather than transformed into a narrative simultaneity. It reminds me of the films of Roger Corman, but in an inverse way.

Andy I've seen some of those. They're pretty to look at.

Bob His films are structured by an aesthetic of atemporality that negates any narrative simultaneity, but it does so by refusing all naturalism. His actors always appear vacant and transparent and simply move through a series of settings or locations. Duration is drained out and we begin to move through networks of an infinite mind. Locations are not presented; instead, they become, as Poe once said, "immeasurable but definite distances."[21]

Andy I guess, but sometimes the bad acting gets to me. No acting is better.

Bob It's a goal, but probably an ideal one, just as expression is.

Andy I guess. But you know, *Chelsea Girls* was really our first breakthrough film, the first one that got shown at a mid-town art house. We did pretty well with it, financially I mean. Everyone said that we'd finally made a real movie.

Bob Yet the disintegration of the film it represents is actually a highly developed condition. The implicit formalism of montage dissolves into a pure temporality. The French anthropologist Claude Lèvi-Strauss suggested we develop a new discipline called "Entropology."[22]

Andy Someday, I think I'd like to make an abstract film, you know, maybe only with objects, like you do, rather than people.[23]

Bob *Chelsea Girls* is more abstract than any abstract painting. Cinema became a harvesting of time and the awareness of an absence rather than the creation of an ever-present now that paradoxically throws us out of time.

Andy But that's what I like about movies. They make you forget about time.

Bob The final scene of *Chelsea Girls*, where Ondine attacks that girl who calls her a phony is pertinent here. The girl was telling the truth because Ondine was trying to own herself through the camera's eye. The girl was only pointing to the fact that the camera had opened a gaping hole in reality that Ondine was trying to cover with glamour. In that sense, we can easily say aura is a surface that hides the void but never lets you forget that it's there. It was one of the truly brilliant moments of film.

Andy Well, thanks, but you know, I really didn't have anything to do with that scene. It kind of just happened, and I didn't really understand why they were getting so worked up. It was so abstract.

Bob It demonstrated that abstraction and nature are merging in art, and that the synthesizer is the camera, which shows nature as something meaningful. When Ondine slaps that girl, you think, "Wow, that was real." Later, you realize it doesn't really mean anything precisely because it was real. Reality is the most abstract thing of all.

Andy Whenever Ondine gets anywhere near real people, bad things happen. That's because whenever she leaves New York she gets confused by all that reality.

Bob We live in frameworks and are surrounded by frames of reference, yet nature dismantles them. *Chelsea Girls* does the same, so I'm not surprised that she gets confused. She's only more honest about it to herself, which is why she acts the way she does.

Andy That's why I like movies. You start out confused, not knowing what's going on, and in a really good movie, you come out the same way.

Bob That's why your films are absolutely confusing: because they don't start out confusing and never confuse you at all. A film is capable of picking up pieces of things, the archeological remains of cultures, but in film they always remain fragments. They never resolve into "culture" or "history," which is what montage inevitably does.[24]

Andy   Maybe we're somehow caught in a movie. Maybe someone is secretly following us around with a camera. Maybe that's why we're so confused.

Bob   Maybe they'll call it *Chelsea Boys*, though you wouldn't be able to see anything.

Andy   That sounds like a movie John Cage would make.

Bob   It does.

Andy   You know, Brigid called this morning, and she was probably lying about the fact that she didn't call me last night to wake me up.

Bob   What are you talking about?

Andy   Someone woke me up in the middle of the night, and I think it was probably Brigid, but she wouldn't admit it. If I were paranoid, I would say you were in on it with her.

Bob   That is paranoid.

Andy   So then where are we? I haven't heard you come up with any good ideas.

Bob   You really want to hear what I think?

Andy   Sure.

Bob   Alright. If we are being filmed, it's only by the Infinite Camera, which lies somewhere between the still and the moving camera.[25]

Andy   Sounds fancy.

Bob You shouldn't think of the Infinite Camera as something real. It's just something to think or write about.[26]

Andy Can it record in the dark?

Bob Just because it's infinite doesn't mean it's all-powerful.

Andy So what does it do?

Bob Working backwards, we could define its basic aspects. If a normal camera records the world around it, the Infinite Camera records what's not in the world.

Andy What's not in the world?

Bob Ideas, for example. Have you ever seen one? We don't even speak of them in those terms. We "have" ideas, we don't see them.

Andy That's true. People have said I have some good ideas, but when I stop to try to see what they are, I can't seem to ever find one.

Bob That's because it's impossible to discover them. One has to produce them. Seeing implies that you know what they look like before you've ever seen one.

Andy Just like stars. You see them on TV, in a Western or something, and you think, "oh, that's so and so, and he's still wearing the same outfit he wore in the last movie."

Bob Think about it in terms of television. Television brings what's far away close, but you can only know what you're seeing if you've already seen it somewhere else. That's why it sticks to formulas. It takes a long time to retrain the audience to recognize something new.

Andy I thought you we were talking about things people can't see?

Bob It's only an analogy, Andy.

Andy Oh. You know, I've got an idea. Maybe we've been somehow turned into ideas, invisible to everyone else besides ourselves, like an episode of *The Twilight Zone*? I did recognize you right away when I first walked into the coffee shop. Everyone in the Factory is probably saying, "Andy went off to see so and so again, and he didn't tell anyone."

Bob I'd put it this way: the Infinite Camera doesn't so much record the invisible as it erases the visible. Like ideas, the infinite isn't something one finds lying around ready to be recorded like one finds earth, rocks, or crystals.

Andy It's not?

Bob The infinite is produced by the Infinite Camera. Instead of recording something that's already there, it makes the finite infinite. It infinitizes.

Andy That sounds very surreal.

Bob And unlike television, which brings far away things close, the infinite is produced by separating things and making space between them, even between ourselves and those things closest to us.

Andy I see. Like when you look through binoculars backward and everything seems so far away.

Bob Yes, but imagine it was so far away you couldn't see it.

Andy I believe in empty spaces. On the other hand, because I'm still making art for people to put in their spaces, the ones I believe should be empty, I'm helping people waste their space when what I really want to do is help them empty it.[27]

Bob You don't practice what you preach.

Andy That's what I'm saying. I breach what I preach more than I practice it.[28]

Bob I wouldn't worry about it now.

Andy Why? Because we're dead?

Bob No, because when I say "space," I don't mean it literally. Tele-in-vision is that in which the "tele," i.e., distance, is in vision itself. If it were literal, you could see it.

Andy I see.

Bob To use an example from what we were talking about earlier, if perspective in painting brings things into vision, the Infinite Camera would take things out of vision because the infinite cannot be visualized.

Andy It would take forever.

Bob Right.

Andy Bob, did anyone ever tell you you talk like no one else in the world?

Bob I try to put distance into words in the same way the Infinite Camera puts the "tele" in vision. But I can say the same thing about you. Your dis-synchronized talk and monosyllabic English are tropistic. They produce unbridgeable distances.[29]

Andy I'd say that's going too far.

Bob Why?

Andy When you say "unbridgeable distance," the only thing I can think of is death. Death is the farthest thing I can imagine, and I should know because I was there, and even when you're there, it's the farthest thing you can imagine. So I guess it means that's where we are.

Bob So what do you propose we do?

Andy I think I'd like to get back to the Factory to do some work.

Bob Work? What for?

Andy Artists should never stop working, especially if they're dead. That's the best thing about fame. You work even after you die, and the more famous you are when you go, the harder you work later. Take Marilyn. She never worked as much while she was alive as she does now that she's dead. When I die—or now that I'm dead—I'm going to work really hard. The minute you stop working, people forget about you.

Bob That seems like a way of trying to stay alive, of not admitting that you're dead. But I'm not ready to admit it either. I'm just not sure.

Andy After I was shot, I was never really sure I was alive again. Everything changed. Before I was shot, watching TV was one of my favorite things to do. Afterward, I started to feel like my life was television. So if we're dead and working, then maybe it's just like being on television.[30]

Bob On television things are "LIVE."

Andy Then maybe we're pre-recorded. Or maybe we're "LIVE," only somewhere else.

Bob What do you mean?

Andy   I mean that being on television is being somewhere else. So maybe if we're on television, we're just somewhere else.

Bob   You're going to have to explain that.

Andy   When you're on TV, your image can be halfway around the world, but not just in one place. You can be in a million places all at once. The more famous you are, the more places you can be all at the same time. *Ultrafame* would be when you're everywhere at once.

Bob   Everywhere?

Andy   Exactly. Don't you think that's why God is so famous?

Bob   You're saying we've become like god, everywhere at once and invisible?

Andy   No, not quite as famous as he is. Not even Mao is that famous.

Bob   If that's the case, then I'll go with your other idea.

Andy   Which one?

Bob   That we're dead. If we're everywhere at once, and so is God, then God is dead too.

Andy   Could be.

Bob   There's one place that you can't record with a camera or a television.

Andy   Where's that?

Bob   The place behind the camera.

Andy   That's where I like to stand.

Bob But you've been in movies. You're in front of the camera all the time.

Andy That's not me. It's just my face.

Bob Godard says that "a camera filming itself in a mirror would be the ultimate movie."[31] The *ne plus ultra* of fame is that fame becomes the most famous thing. In other words, we're still talking about Vertov's ideas about film when we talk about television. In both, the camera becomes subject and object at the same time, the worker and the star of the show. And Godard knew that was impossible.

Andy Why's that?

Bob A camera filming itself filming is filming nothing.

Andy Nothing could be interesting.

Bob Only formally.

Andy It doesn't hurt to try.

Bob I once thought about making a piece called *Underground Cinema*. It would be a theater, but the only film it would show would be one of its own construction, how it was dug and hollowed out of the ground. Instead of a camera seeing itself, it would be a space spacing itself, a document of its own future. The moment the cave was complete would also be the end of the film.

Andy That sounds fascinating. Did you ever make it?

Bob It's an impossible proposition. The subject of the film, the cave, only comes to be after the film is finished. It means that the film is filming what is in fact a future that hasn't arrived yet, and which arrives at precisely the moment it stops recording. When you can finally see the film, you're seeing a past that doesn't belong to the present.

Andy I think that's what love is like. You're working toward it thinking you're about to get there, but by the time you do, you're already trying to recapture it because you think it's gone and you want to get it back. That's how it always is on soap operas.

Bob Right, and love lives in that separation between past and future. Television abolishes that experience of time and throws everything into an absolute present. Vertov never confronted this problem. He thought the camera could negate time by making it all one and the same era, the historical era of revolution. The truth is Futurism was more interested in the present than in the future, and we still haven't figured out how to be true Futurists.

Andy I'm beginning to think that that's what we're doing now. Whether we're dead or not, we're going to have to start living for the future. I just wonder what I'm going to do.

Bob A television signal traverses space when in transmission, so there's always going to be at least a microsecond delay—like the blink of an eye. For Vertov's idea to work, the camera would need to see its own blink. It brings us into paradoxes that are more than just logical.

Andy I remember a critic—he was German, I think—who kept saying I was full of contradictions and paradoxes. He kept asking me questions, and I just didn't know what to say. It was like someone had glued my mouth shut.

Bob Why do you think that happened?

Andy I guess because I was worried he was right, and I didn't want to give him the satisfaction. Usually, I don't have a problem with contradictions or paradoxes.

Bob You've opened a yawning abyss more terrifying than any logical contradiction of philosophical paradox.

Andy In a hundred years, he might end up here with us, and I'd have something to say.

Bob When I see your films, I see people who are all dead to me even though I know they're alive. By removing the interval, you've demonstrated that it's never merely a formal device, a compositional tool. Actually, it's not unique to the moving picture. It's internal to every image.

Andy Someone once told me that my films were like being forced to stare at a photograph for eight hours.

Bob Photography possesses perhaps the purest interval of them all, but one related to the past. The moving picture's interval is directed to the future. Television tries to manipulate it and put it to work by promising what's "coming up, right after these messages."

Andy What's coming up is usually disappointing. Then I settle into my disappointment and start to enjoy it.

Bob My point is that by holding us in a perpetual present always promising what's "coming up," it steals the future and the past as well. The present is never allowed to pass away. The real message is "stay where you are and don't move, and whatever you do, never forget that I, the present, am always here." It arrests you.

Andy Maybe that's why I can never turn it off. I sit there for hours thinking, "okay, something is going to happen now." And it does, but by then I'm already waiting for the next thing thinking "okay, something is going to happen now." And I can't remember what happened five minutes ago. That is, until I woke up this morning. Now I can't forget anything. Do you want me to tell you what we said ten minutes ago?

Bob That's not necessary. I believe you. It's pretty remarkable, though it doesn't seem to be related to death, which, you would think, is the total forgetting of everything.

Andy Isn't that just what we were saying about television.

Bob In a different way. With television, the transmission happens before you ever see what you're waiting for.

Andy How's that?

Bob It's you who is really being transmitted, delivered to advertisers as so many "viewers like yourself." The program is just the lure. The true sense of television fame, what Vertov imagined as the ideal mechanism of the revolutionary society always connecting individuals through the eye of the camera, is that viewers are made famous only as aggregates and masses, in the numerical language of money found in the pages of corporate reports.

Andy Well, everyone knows that.

Bob True, but far worse is the fact that, paradoxically, the present becomes a pure waiting. People sit around waiting for something to happen, and if it doesn't happen on television, it doesn't register as an event. Television suspends the future in a perpetual present, and if it comes, it can only come as a catastrophe that interrupts the daily series of programs.

Andy Do you think we've become somehow suspended? Maybe only some kind of catastrophe can shake us out of here.
Bob I just don't know. Perhaps we've just been swallowed by television's distanceless distance.

Andy In the 50s, I'd been hurt a lot—to the degree you can only be hurt if you care a lot. When I got my first TV set, I stopped caring about having close relationships with other people. I started to have distanced relationships, even with my friends.[32]

Bob Distance preserves a thing's aura by doing away with its specific character in the same way that fame destroys the specific personality of stars, turning them slowly into copies of themselves. We need a distance that isn't easily reproducible or that must be reproduced each time, just as the Infinite Camera reproduces invisibilities.

Andy Maybe Duchamp was right when he said that, the only way that remains open for art is to go "underground." That's distant. Isn't that what Oldenburg did?

Bob Maybe, but the cube isn't buried very deep.

Andy Well, you also don't know exactly where it is. If you want to know what I think, underground art has the aura of aura.

Bob The aura of aura?

Andy You can't tell when someone with the aura of aura really has aura or doesn't. That's when they really get distance. You look into their eyes and there's just nothing there. To be honest, that's what Duchamp seemed like.

Bob Maybe that was just a language boundary.

Andy No, it was like he really was not there.

Bob That's interesting. People say that a lot about you.

Andy I know.

Bob I've never believed it. You're more there than most people.

Andy Sure.

Bob In any case, going "underground" doesn't seem like much of a solution. It can only ever be the next step in the history of art. It is a *de facto* confinement. Land art and my earth works were attempts to get out of the gallery and the studio and the entire art system. Even above ground, they were trying to be "underground."

Andy Did it work out?

Bob You can't will it "to work out." What's happening is that art is increasingly migrating to film and television and even land art is surrendering to it, either as the "closed landscape" in which units of land are measured and we get the equivalent of something like an "object," or the "open landscape," which tries to embody multiple points of view, some of which may be contradictory, and whose purpose is to reveal the clash of angles and orders within the simultaneity of a single work.[33]

Andy Even your work?

Bob I try to make it impossible to screen by putting it in touch with language. If the closed landscape is a matter of faith and certainty, the open landscape is a matter of skepticism and uncertainty. Language permits both interpretations, and therefore safeguards its distance.

Andy If both were true, which one do you choose?

Bob It's not a choice. If it were, you'd be tossed right back into the present again. It's more like a fate.

Andy Well, then some day you'll know which one it is.

Bob Someday will take forever to come.

Andy Then it's like it has the aura of aura. If you ask me, that's the real fate of fame. Maybe it's already happened, and fame is over. What would New York be without fame?

Bob I have no idea.

Andy I don't either, but maybe that's fame.

Bob Instead of thinking of fame as being suspended, think of it as "hovering" over the present, separate from it. Not in the future, but turned toward it.

Andy What are we going to do without fame? It'll be just like being in here all the time, like someone turned off all the lights.

Bob I don't mind. Aren't you curious to know what darkness *is*?

Andy What do you mean? How can you be curious about what you can't see? I'm curious about green bills.[34]

Bob My underground cinema was meant to be an anti-monument, an impossible monument to the future, because the past has always passed away. In passing away, it has succeeded in preserving the future.

Andy So then we're not dead? Everyone just left? What am I going to do now?

Bob Some day, artists and critics might finally understand that every true history, every image of the past, is an entropy of the future. The point of art and art history would be to discover and describe this trope. That's the only way they could become truly historical.

Andy You think so?

Bob The future can only arrive if we can be done with history, the past, as our present.

Andy That sounds like a film of something that succeeds in not happening. It happens not to happen.

Bob Or you could say that something happens in appearing not to happen.

Andy What's the difference?

Bob In the first, something doesn't happen. In the second, it only appears to not happen but actually happens.

Andy If it doesn't happen, then the future remains in the future.

Bob Exactly. But if it only appears to not happen, the future sneaks up on us like a spy. It happens, but no one notices, and we go on thinking nothing has changed.

Andy Does that mean we're futurists?

Bob I don't know.

Andy Maybe we've already been thrown into your new future, the one that happens in appearing not to happen.

Bob It's possible.

Andy So it's just a matter of describing this future? That doesn't sound too hard, since we're already here. I'm going to describe it exactly as it happened. I remember every word.

Bob You'd have to become a writer, and you hate to write. Don't expect it to be as profitable as business art.

Andy I'm going to describe it exactly as it happened. I remember every word. I've already written my philosophy and my novel. This will be my autobiography.

Bob Of the future?

Andy Sure. And when I'm finished writing everything down, I'll try to remember everything else.

Bob I thought you had a terrible memory.

Andy That's true. But if things go on like this, all I have is time. I was starting to get used to the idea of being dead. If we're in the future, I better get ready.

Bob It's an interesting idea, Andy, but you'd still have to think about dying.

Andy I think that I don't want to leave any leftovers when I die. I was watching TV once and I saw a lady go into a ray machine and disappear. That was wonderful because matter is energy and she just dispersed. That could be the best American invention—to be able to disappear.[35]

Bob That would definitely be the future, don't you think?

Andy Sure.

Notes

Empire

[1]
Robert Smithson, in *Robert Smithson: The Collected Writings*, (Berkeley: University of California Press, 1996), p.11. All further references to Smithson, unless otherwise indicated, refer to this volume.

[2]
Andy Warhol, *The Philosophy of Andy Warhol (From A to B and Back Again)*, (New York: Harcourt, Brace & Company, New York, 1975), p. 156.

[3]
Smithson, p. 341.

[4]
Ibid., p. 63.

[5]
Warhol, p. 109.

[6]
Smithson, p. 52.

[7]
Ibid., p. 361.

Central Park

[1]
Warhol, p. 181.

[2]
Ibid.

[3]
Smithson, p. 48.

[4]
Warhol, p. 148.

[5]
Ibid., p. 147, 148.

[6]
Ibid., p. 74.

[7]
Ibid., p. 195.

[8]
Ibid., p. 50.

[9]
Ibid., p. 112.

[10]
Ibid., p. 44.

[11]
Ibid., p. 44.

[12]
Ibid., p. 74.

[13]
This is, according to Smithson, Carl Andre's motto. See Smithson, "A Thing is a Hole in a Thing it is Not," p. 95.

[14]
Smithson, p. 74.

[15]
Ibid., p. 74.

[16]
Ibid., p. 337, 338.

[17]
Ibid.

[18]
Ibid.

[19]
Ibid., p. 338.

[20]
Ibid.

[21]
Warhol, p. 113.

Underground Cinema

[1]
Smithson, p. 135.

[2]
Ibid., p. 311.

[3]
Ibid.

[4]
Ibid.

[5]
Ibid.

[6]
Ibid., p. 197.

[7]
Warhol, p. 147.

[8]
Smithson, p. 66, 67.

[9]
Warhol, p. 26.

[10]
Ibid., p. 77.

[11]
Ibid., p. 80.

[12]
Ibid., p. 81.

[13]
Ibid., p. 61 and p. 83, 841.

[14]
Ibid., p. 80.

[15]
Ibid., p. 49, 50.

[16]
Ibid., p. 98.

[17]
Ibid., p. 66, 67.

[18]
Ibid., p. 80, 81.

[19]
Ibid., p. 372.

[20]
Ibid.

[21]
Ibid., p. 90.

[22]
Ibid., p. 375.

[23]
Ibid., p. 371.

[24]
Ibid., p. 374.

[25]
Ibid., p. 372.

[26]
Ibid.

[27]
Warhol, p. 144.

[28]
Ibid., p. 144.

[29]
Smithson, p. 82.

[30]
Ibid., p. 91.

[31]
Smithson, p. 141.

[32]
Warhol, p. 26.

[33]
Smithson, p. 374.

[34]
Warhol, p. 129.

DOCUMENTS – DOCUMENTS SERIES 1
Saul Anton

This book is the first volume in "Documents – Documents Series,"
dedicated to english publication of critics' writings.

The series is directed by Lionel Bovier and Xavier Douroux.

Available:

DOCUMENTS – DOCUMENTS SERIES

Saul Anton, *Warhol's Dream*, 2007
Les presses du réel : 978-2-84066-200-6
JRP|Ringier : 978-3-905770-35-3

Bob Nickas, *Theft is Vision*, 2007
Les presses du réel : 978-2-84066-206-8
JRP|Ringier : 978-3-905770-36-0

DOCUMENTS – DOCUMENTS SUR L'ART

Daniel Birnbaum, *Chronologie*, 2007
Les presses du réel : 978-2-84066-165-8
JRP|Ringier : 978-3-905770-98-8

Diedrich Diedrichsen, *Argument son*, 2007
Les presses du réel : 978-2-84066-140-5
JRP|Ringier : 978-3-905829-00-6

Edited by Xavier Douroux

Proofreading: Clare Manchester and Rachel Urkowitz
Design: Patricia Bobillier-Monnot
Design Concept: Gilles Gavillet
Headline Typeface: Genath by David Dust & Gilles Gavillet

ACKNOWLEDGMENTS:
The author would like to express his gratitude to the following people, who have each in their own way made this book possible: Cletus Daglish-Somer, Julie Carson, Sina Najafi, Benjamin Lytal, Lytle Shaw, and Rachel Urkowitz.
The author would also like to thank the following people and institutions for their kind support of this project: Nancy Holt, Elyse Goldberg, the Estate of Robert Smithson.

An early version of "Empire" originally appeared in *Cabinet* magazine.

PUBLISHED BY:
Les presses du réel
16, rue Quentin
F–21000 Dijon
T +33 3 80 30 75 23
F +33 3 80 30 59 74
E info@lespressesdureel.com
www.lespressesdureel.com

IN CO-EDITION WITH:
JRP|Ringier
Letzigraben 134
CH–8047 Zurich
T +41 43 311 227 50
F +41 43 311 27 51
E info@jrp-ringier.com
www.jrp-ringier.com

DISTRIBUTION:

France
Les presses du réel, 16 rue Quentin, F-21000 Dijon
info@lespressesdureel.com, www.lespressesdureel.com

Switzerland
Buch 2000, AVA Verlagsauslieferung AG, Centralweg 16, CH-8910 Affoltern a.A.
buch2000@ava.ch, www.ava.ch

Germany and Austria
Vice Versa Vertrieb, Immanuelkirchestrasse 12, D-10405 Berlin
info@vice-versa-vertrieb.de, www.vice-versa-vertribe.de

UK
Art Data, 12 Bell Industrial Estate, 50 Cunnington Street, London W4 5HB
info@artdata.co.uk, www.ardata.co.uk

USA
D.A.P. / Distributed Art Publisher, 155 Sixth Avenue, 2nd Floor, New York, NY 10013
dap@dapinc.com, www.artbook.com

Other countries
Idea Books, Nieuwe Herengracht 11, NL-1011 RK Amsterdam
idea@ideabooks.nl, www.ideabooks.nl

Achevé d'imprimer sur rotative par l'imprimerie Darantiere
à Dijon-Quetigny en juillet 2007 – Imprimé en France
Dépôt légal : 3ᵉ trimestre 2007 – Nᵒ d'impression : 271139